PSYCHIC POWER:

How To Develop Your ESP

BY RICHARD DeA'MORELLI

BOOKS FOR BETTER LIVING • CHATSWORTH, CALIFORNIA

To my wife, Cathy, for her patience, understanding and gentle persuasion to finish this book.

They said, "What sign can you give us to see, so that we may believe you?"

John 6: 30-31

CONTENTS

Chapter One

Telepathy: Secrets of Mental Communication

Is it possible for a person in Los Angeles to communicate *mentally* with someone in, say, New York or Miami?

Before you dismiss the idea of mind reading as a hoax, consider these facts: Thousands of people have reported genuine experiences with mental communication to prestigious organizations such as the American Society for Psychical Research. And at Duke University, a team of scientists working under the direction of Dr. Joseph B. Rhine, world-famous psychic pioneer, has spent years engaged in laboratory experiments to determine the validity of mind reading. The evidence conclusively shows that telepathy exists!

Now consider this: The Russians have been investigating the psychic realm since 1962. Based on the findings of Soviet scientists, the government is so convinced that mental communication and other phenomena can be produced at will, it is pouring billions of dollars into top secret research to find out how telepathy works and how it may be put to use for social and military objectives. No less than ten notable institutes are officially sponsoring ESP experiments and training centers, the best known being Leningrad University, where an impressively credentialed team of biologists, psychologists, neurologists, physicists, physicians and mathematicians are hard at work training psychics and delving into the mysteries of the human mind.

You may not realize it, but every man and woman alive was born with ESP traits. You and I are free to unlock the vast reservoir of psychic energy which lies dormant in our minds. Through our sixth sense we may add a wonderful new dimension to our lives and realize our every secret ambition.

Think of it: Through the power of mind reading, you can know the thoughts of friends and acquaintances. You can perceive your employer's desires and so gain rapid recognition. This amazing power can add a new dimension to your love life, enabling you to converse mentally with your mate and know his or her needs and desires. And even though you may be miles away from your friends and loved ones, you can communicate with them just as though you were seated in the same room.

The Telepathic Development Program outlined in this chapter is a simple step-by-step course which teaches you how to unlock these hidden powers and use them in daily living. There are no gimmicks or dangers involved, no drugs or stimulants of any kind required. The program is based on natural principles and can be mastered easily by anyone willing to spend a few minutes every day performing the fascinating experiments and growth exercises which have been included.

The Telepathic Development Program, which is the first section of a comprehensive curriculum called the Psychic Development Program (PDP), was originally assembled in 1970 through the joint efforts of myself and several colleagues including Genia Hastur and Michael O'Brien, both of whom have assisted me in my psychic endeavors on a multitude of occasions, and my wife, Catherine, who is a highly developed psychic in her own right. Standard procedures developed by Dr. Rhine are incorporated in the format along with popular metaphysical and occult tenets. The result is a thorough and comprehensive course in personal ESP development.

Whether you are a devout believer in mind-to-mind communication and want to cultivate this power, or merely hold a passing interest in the subject is of no consequence. Skeptics have applied this program and realized amazing results. It does help, of course, to have an open mind, but it is not absolutely necessary. By the time you finish this chapter, you will not only be convinced that you possess telepathic powers, but you will probably be using mental communication as a regular part of your life. And that is the whole idea behind this book.

So let us begin with the fundamentals.

TELEPATHY DEFINED

Telepathy is the most rudimentary psychic power man possesses. It is reported more frequently than any other form of ESP and is also the easiest to master. Often, it is called mental communication, mind reading and thought transference. Telepathy may be used voluntarily by every man, woman and child, and it is entirely safe when properly (and discreetly) applied. It has nothing to do with witchcraft, fortune-telling or commercialized mystic religions.

Telepathy in its pure form involves: 1) receiving and correctly interpreting another person's thoughts, and 2) transmitting mental messages with sufficient intensity so that they will be perceived clearly by the intended recipient.

The power of mind-to-mind communication is divided into two general classifications: spontaneous and controlled. The first term refers to those experiences which occur without conscious effort. Crisis, emotional stress and exhaustion usually trigger the phenomena, especially between close friends and loved ones who are in grave danger.

Conversely, controlled telepathy is produced voluntarily by an individual and may be turned on and off at will. No adverse mental or physical conditions need exist. Through a series of mental exercises designed to activate the sixth sense, the power of telepathy may be used at any time of the day and in any environment.

COMMON MYTHS

Factors of age, race and gender have no true bearing on one's telepathic abilities. Granted, young people, 12 to 26-year-olds, do obtain significantly higher scores on ESP tests, but this trend is principally due to the fact that older people were taught to repress their psychic potential and mistrust anything which smacks of spiritualism or the supernatural.

Likewise, the truism that women are more psychically powerful than men does not always seem to be the case. In fact, there are some males of my own acquaintance who are much more psychic than their female counterparts. Yet, here again, females do score generally higher on ESP tests primarily due to social and cultural conditioning. To wit, feminine intuition and, for the most part, sensitivity in women happen to be socially acceptable, particularly in America. But in men, this same gentleness is condemned and viewed as a weakness. Quite mistakenly, some men who demonstrate acute *awareness* and overall sensitivity are considered dull and, at worst, effeminate. Hence, the need to repress any and all of these supposedly "female" qualities accounts for the apparent psychic superiority of females.

In reality, telepathy is a perfectly natural function of the human brain, just as the remaining *five* senses—*sight, smell, hearing, taste and touch*—are natural. People of all races, both sexes, the young and old have been equally successful in the use of controlled telepathy.

You may rest assured that you were born with just as much psychic potential as the world's leading seers. The only difference is that they have already learned how to make use of their hidden psychic powers.

MENTAL ELECTRICITY

The power of mind reading functions in much the same way as the human eye sees tangible objects and color. In visual perception, light vibrations pass through the pupil, striking the retina and transmitting an exact image to the visual cortex in the brain. Telepathy operates according to the same basic principle; however, in lieu of light vibrations, mental communication involves the registration and interpretation of psychic impulses reacting upon thought-sensitive brain centers.

Parapsychologists have long theorized that thought in its purest state consists of electrical energy, but it was not until comparatively recent times that substantiating evidence emerged. Now we know that brain waves are indeed electrical and that they can be measured by any one of several sensitive laboratory devices. Science has found ways to record the intensity of a person's thoughts and to determine mental incapacities solely by the use of a complicated electronic system which is attached to the body. Another sensitive instrument is used to record a person's dream patterns during sleep. Similar equipment is now in the experimental stages; indeed one device may soon make it possible to record your exact thoughts and, through a computerized process, symbolically interpret them!

As the result of such technological breakthroughs, we have come to realize that telepathy involves the transmission of mental electricity from one mind to another. We all constantly generate these psychic impulses: We can learn to channel our own mental electricity and make our brain more receptive to impulses being transmitted by other people.

The challenge then is to train the mind to act as a two-way radio system complete with on-off switch, volume control and fine tuning. This, of course, is the purpose of the Telepathic Development Program: to show the fundamental principles, applications and rich potential you can enjoy by unlocking and using this amazing power in daily life.

PRACTICAL APPLICATIONS
OF TELEPATHY

Exactly what is the value of mind reading? How can this unusual mental power be employed to your best advantage? These questions are frequently asked by people from all walks of life. Unfortunately, most books on ESP devote only minimal space to answering these pertinent issues and the average reader therefore comes to think of psychic power as a novelty with no real use.

So, why should you waste your time and energy cultivating your telepathic powers if they are nothing more than the source of minor entertainment?

There are, in fact, many practical applications but space does not permit their listing. However, there are for learning how to use telepathy five popular reasons which do warrant attention.

First, mind reading will let you know what strangers and new acquaintances are thinking and how they really feel about you. Second, you will be better able to understand the hidden thoughts, feelings and motives of your friends, your relatives and loved ones, your contemporaries and business partners. Third, telepathic power will enable you to establish a more meaningful and stable love relationship by strengthening the emotional and spiritual bonds which bind you.

Fourth, you can attract recognition and advancement in all your career pursuits. You will automatically know how to please and impress your employer, make a favorable impression on potential employers and new co-workers, even find out when to change jobs and what profession to engage in for greatest success.

Finally, through a power known as distance telepathy, you will be able to communicate with friends and loved ones who may be travelling or residing in another city or state. Needless to say, distance telepathy is more economical than a phone call, less time-consuming than writing a letter, and by far more intimate than other conventional forms of communication.

These five general examples should give you a basic idea as to the real value of telepathic powers. As you learn how to cultivate and apply these abilities, you will probably find a multitude of other applications not mentioned above but just as important to your personal success and happiness.

A FASCINATING EXPERIMENT

Here is an interesting, easy-to-perform experiment designed to demonstrate the simplicity and effectiveness of telepathic power. Also, it may help to convince those of you who remain skeptical that mental communication is not just an imaginary occurrence.

At a busy hour during the day, go to a park, a restaurant or some other public place where a crowd of people will be present. If you choose to conduct this experiment in a restaurant, seat yourself at an empty booth near a stranger. If you go to a park, select a person who will be your passive and unsuspecting subject. Station yourself about ten to thirty yards away from your chosen subject (fifty yards away if you are in a park or other open space). Regardless of your location, you must position yourself so that the subject will be seated with his or her back toward you.

Now, concentrate your full attention on the person's neck just at the base of the skull. Do not attempt to send a particular thought at first. Just gaze intently at the designated area for about one minute. Then, when your concentration is at peak efficiency, broadcast this mental command: "You will turn around and look at me ..." Silently form each word carefully in your mind and send the message to your subject with intensity. But do not interrupt your visual concentration in the process. Continue repeating the phrase, slowly and forcefully, for about one minute or less.

Either the experiment will fail completely, or you will encounter success to some degree. To evaluate the results of this particular test, here are a few simple guidelines to follow:

If, at the end of a full minute or two, your subject has not responded to your mental command and continues to appear completely unaffected, do not be discouraged. This merely indicates that your power of concentration is low and requires development. As stated before, everyone can master telepathy; some people are more naturally adapted to the use of their sixth sense than others. Follow the practical guidelines outlined in this chapter and perform all the growth and concentration exercises. Then try this same experiment again and I guarantee that you will be successful.

It may be that your power of concentration is already developed to a limited degree. You may therefore find that the experiment was a partial success. Many times, a beginner will lack sufficient power to actually make his or her subject respond. Yet the subject may begin squirming nervously or scratching at the back of the neck due to a sudden sensation of discomfort triggered by your intense mental command. If you succeed in evoking such a response, your telepathic powers are probably more developed than you suspect.

There is always a chance that your power of concentration is already highly refined, even though you may not be consciously aware of it. If your subject turns around and glances at you with an unpleasant expression on his face (which he or she most likely will not understand), the experiment has been a complete success. Congratulate yourself, then proceed to the following passages without delay.

PERFECT RELAXATION: HOW TO UNLOCK YOUR POWER OF TELEPATHY

As you have just seen from the preceeding experiment, the ability to focus the mind on a specific desire, thought or object is the key to telepathic power. Unless you know how to concentrate, it will be virtually impossible to transmit or receive thoughts with sufficient clarity and intensity. Noise, movement, physical discomfort and other minor distractions will inevitably interfere with any attempt at mental communication.

The power of concentration—or single-mindedness, as the Hindus call it—is not something that can be developed overnight. It takes practice and more practice, but once you master the technique, your psychic powers will rapidly unfold.

There are numerous approaches to the cultivation of single-mindedness, some more complicated and time-consuming than others. The method discussed here is probably the easiest and most worthwhile. However, it is important to understand that this technique (as well as all others) relies heavily on one particular ingredient: complete relaxation. Once you learn to subdue your mind and body, concentration will automatically follow.

Learning to relax is not as easy as most people seem to think. You might be convinced that you have reached perfect relaxation when you stop working and sit down to rest. But this is nothing more than a change of routine. In reality, if you are like most men and women, you are no more relaxed—even when sleeping—than you are while at work or at a party. Your thoughts are still racing, your mind churns with anxiety and your muscles are tense. Problems, fears and apprehension about the future all flash in and out of your mind.

This is not perfect relaxation. The desired state is not automatically reached, even in sleep. (Very few people, in fact, get a good night's rest because they do not know how to actually relax and rid the mind of worry, a condition obviously reflected by the unsettling dreams and feeling of exhaustion most of us experience upon waking.)

Perfect relaxation must be consciously cultivated and practiced. To achieve it, the mind must be subdued and tranquil, void of all thoughts. Further, every muscle in the body must be completely relaxed, otherwise, minor physical discomforts will provide an endless string of distractions, rendering telepathy impossible.

If you want to find out just how tense and active you are while supposedly relaxing, make yourself comfortable in a quiet room and try this experiment:

Lean back, close your eyes and visualize a green circle in your mind's eye. Be sure that all the lines are clear and bright. Now, hold this image for about five minutes without it fading, disappearing or flickering.

You can't do it, right? After five or ten seconds, you probably found that it was extremely difficult to maintain a constant image of the symbol. Your mind began to wander, your body grew restless and finally the image faded completely.

Don't be discouraged if this happened: At least ninety-five percent of the people who take this test for the first time cannot maintain a clear image of the circle for more than ten or fifteen seconds without physical or mental interference.

Needless to say, if you have trouble concentrating on a simple image, you cannot realistically hope to use your telepathic power without encountering similar difficulty. The crux of the situation then revolves around the inability to relax.

In perfect relaxation, your mind is blank, your muscles are not tense and distractions in your surroundings do not prove to be disturbing. An individual who has mastered perfect relaxation does not hear or see sounds and movements, even though other people nearby may react to these external conditions. At this stage, concentration power is at a peak and telepathic communication is easily accomplished.

RELAXATION EXERCISE NO. 1

How does one master the art of perfect relaxation?

Here is a three-step technique for cultivating the desired state of mind. After these exercises have been performed for about one week, you will be able to achieve perfect relaxation in just a few seconds, no matter where you are, without anyone even noticing.

To begin with, choose a room in your home where you can be completely alone for ten or fifteen minutes every day. Select a quiet place free from all distractions. For best results, the room should be cool and as dark as possible, well-ventilated so that the air is not too humid. Turn off all the lights and draw the curtains. Be sure that the radio, record player and television are turned off, as these noise-producers will only hinder your progress.

As to clothing, you should wear only those articles which are absolutely necessary. Warm clothes and garments that are tight-fitting or that restrict your movement in any way should be avoided. Remove all jewelry, headbands, necklaces and rings from your fingers so that these will not be a source of potential distraction.

The ideal position for perfect relaxation is to be seated in a comfortable armchair with your feet elevated on a stool or another chair. This will prevent your blood from going to your feet, and it also provides maximum physical comfort throughout the exercise.

When ready, allow your body to go limp, starting with your legs and moving upward to the abdomen, shoulders, arms, then, finally, to your face. Close your eyes and breathe in deeply and slowly, counting to ten as you do so. Then hold your breath for three counts. Exhale slowly, again to the count of ten, gently forcing the stale air from your lungs. Always breathe through the nostrils, not the mouth.

If you are doing this exercise correctly, the hair in your nose should not vibrate. If it does, breathe more slowly and steadily to correct the condition.

Inhale, then exhale again in this fashion until the breathing exercise has been correctly performed three or four times, then resume your normal breathing pattern and relax for a few seconds.

RELAXATION EXERCISE NO. 2

By this point you have attained a state of light relaxation. Your breathing should be stable and unrestricted, your muscles no longer tense. Proceed as follows:

Contract every muscle in your body. Start with your feet, then move upward to the legs, abdomen, chest, shoulders, arms and, lastly, the face. If you perform this part of Step 2 correctly, every muscle in your body should now be contracted. If you feel uncomfortable, this is perfectly natural. Hold this tension for a count of ten, then gradually let your body go limp again.

Now focus your attention on your toes: Feel every toe on your right foot slowly relaxing. Then concentrate on the left foot. Proceed upward very slowly to the legs, stomach, chest, shoulders and arms. Feel every nerve in your body relaxing and tingling with pleasant sensation of lightness. Follow this same procedure to relax your neck, the muscles of your face and scalp. Enjoy the overall sensation of being completely relaxed for about one minute, or until you have become adjusted to the feeling.

RELAXATION EXERCISE NO. 3

Your mind should now be blank, your body relaxed, as you approach the ultimate state of perfect relaxation.

Now, imagine that you are rising slowly into the air. Feel yourself floating in a black void, drifting on a soothing cushion of warm air. Concentrate on nothing but this pleasant sensation. Soon you will begin to experience a complete lightness, almost as though your body has become weightless. When this occurs, imagine yourself being gently lowered to the ground again. Drift lower and lower until you make contact with the earth.

Gently, open your eyes and remain seated as you are familiarizing yourself with the serene, pleasant state of relaxation which you have attained. Then resume your normal activities.

PROGRESS CHECK

This three-step program should be performed daily without fail so that your mind and body will be more responsive to future sessions. Each time you strive to achieve perfect relaxation, you will find that the desired state comes more naturally and with less effort. It will be easier for you to eliminate all thought from your mind and to relax your body. Also, you will find that the amount of time required to reach perfect relaxation becomes less with each attempt.

Naturally, the first time you perform the exercises will be the most difficult and may consume up to twenty minutes. But, providing you carried out each step correctly on the first day, it will only require about ten minutes to accomplish the same result on the next day. And on the third day, perfect relaxation will come in six or seven minutes; on the following day, in even less time than that.

In a week to ten days, you should be able to complete the entire series of exercises in less than one minute. With further practice, perfect relaxation will come naturally in a few seconds at most. You will be able to relax your body and mind no matter where you are—at work, at school, in your home or while traveling. Surprisingly enough, the presence of other people will not interfere with your trend of thought and no one will even know what you are doing. Other factors which would have annoyed you previously—noise, weather conditions, physical discomfort and external movement—suddenly seem non-existent. You'll find that perfect relaxation is even possible in the midst of a noisy rush hour crowd.

And you'll be well on the way to making use of your telepathic powers!

HOW TO DEVELOP
TELEPATHIC SENSITIVITY

Once you have mastered the art of perfect relaxation, you will be able to transmit and receive thoughts from other people with relative ease. Yet learning to relax is just the first of several steps required for cultivating your telepathic powers.

As you now know, the purpose of perfect relaxation is to subdue the mind and body so that psychic vibrations may be "heard" above the din of one's own thoughts. However, there is more to mind reading—tranquility does not automatically lead to proficiency.

For example, some people—and perhaps yourself—have experienced brief encounters with mind-to-mind communication immediately after performing the perfect relaxation exercises for the first few times. Yet such incidents are usually vague, not at all a true reflection of actual mind reading. But once you are experienced at perfect relaxation you may find yourself able to send and receive thoughts even though you have had no formal training. However, unless you develop one important quality, your telepathic transmissions are liable to be weak, the psychic impulses you receive from other people hazy and garbled. The necessary ingredient is: *telepathic sensitivity*.

Exactly what is telepathic sensitivity? According to definition, it is a state of acute psychic awareness which has vital importance in mental communication as well as all other extrasensory functions. In other words, it is a condition of the mind, much like perfect relaxation. Your brain becomes more sensitive to thought waves emitted by other people. You are better able to "tune in" on friends—or strangers for that matter—and eliminate all static and other interference just as you would get clearer reception by adjusting the tuning knob on a radio.

Telepathic sensitivity enables you to focus and clearly broadcast your own thoughts to anyone in any part of the world, no matter what the recipient's level of personal development happens to be at the time. Likewise, it lends clarity to those thoughts you receive, so that even the weak impulses can come through loud and clear in your mind. This quality also allows you a greater margin of control over mind-to-mind communication. Just as the on-off switch of a radio determines its overall operation, you simply click the dial to the desired position.

Telepathic sensitivity is not a God-given gift as some contemporary psychics insist. It can be developed quickly and easily, without elaborate preparation, through a series of simple practice exercises outlined below.

Where do you begin?

PSYCHIC CURRENTS IN THE HUMAN BODY

First, it is important that you familiarize yourself with the basic principles of the phenomenon of contact telepathy. Also called touch telepathy, this is the most rudimentary of all telepathic powers.

You have already learned that the human brain is a vast reservoir of psychic energy, and that each of us generates thought impulses—brain waves. No matter where we are or what we may be doing, we all produce this mental electricity, even while sleeping.

You may also know that the human body is a natural conductor of electricity. It is therefore reasonable that your body would be saturated by the same psychic energy produced by the brain. These currents of mental electricity may be transmitted to another person solely through physical interaction.

In contact telepathy, thought impulses are conveyed from body to body, rather than from mind to mind, but the end result is invariably the same: You read a person's thoughts just by touching him. What happens, in effect, is that you absorb a portion of the mental electricity in an individual's body. This energy immediately travels through your own body and registers in the mind. Automatically, the thought impulse passes through a process of subconscious interpretation, the end product being valid thought transference.

Needless to say, touch telepathy may be highly valuable when properly employed. Of course, discretion is a must, for you can't go around grabbing at everyone you meet. But, with practice, you can learn to read someone's mind through a mere handshake, a brush of the shoulder or "accidental" contact with the hand or arm.

What follows is an experiment in contact telepathy. Try it and see for yourself just how useful this power can be!

AN EXPERIMENT IN TOUCH TELEPATHY

To carry out this experiment you will need the cooperation of a friend, preferably someone who believes and is interested in psychic phenomena. Retire to a quiet room free from distractions and make yourselves comfortable. Have your friend relax; at the same time, place yourself in the state of perfect relaxation.

Instruct your friend to concentrate on a particular emotion; however, make sure that he or she does not give you any hint as to the selected feeling. For example, if anger is chosen, your partner should recall an incident in the past which evoked intense rage. Once this is done, have your partner close his eyes and concentrate intently on the exact sensation evoked by the memory.

When ready, take your partner's left hand into your own right one. Maintain this contact until you are certain that you have established mental communication. This will probably happen in about one minute. The contact may then be terminated and your impressions checked for accuracy.

In this experiment, you will probably experience an unusual sensation beginning in your hand and moving upward toward the brain. This feeling may be a warmth or a tingling, signaling that your partner's thought impulses are flowing into your own body and to the thought-sensitive areas of your brain. Once this energy reaches your head, the emotion being experienced by your partner should register immediately.

The first time you attempt this experiment, you may have difficulty discerning the exact emotion being transmitted. Any telepathic impression you receive is liable to be hazy and elusive. If your concentration is up to par—and you have in fact mastered perfect relaxation—your interpretation should be nonetheless accurate. After you have tried the same experiment several times, you'll discover that your partner's thoughts begin to register more clearly and that the amount of time required to tune in becomes less.

With a bit more practice, you'll be able to tune in with amazing clarity in just a second or two. The more you practice, the more proficient you become.

If possible, you should enlist the aid of a friend who is interested in psychic development and practice with him or her several times a week, more or less often depending on your own interest level and time schedule. Establish definite times and places to meet and practice. This way, you'll be able to perform the following practice exercises, all of which require the participation of two people.

If you cannot find an interested person, you may still take advantage of every opportunity to exercise your new-found power. Use contact telepathy whenever you shake hands, when among close friends and family, or when walking in a crowd.

Here are five fascinating growth exercises which will prove most valuable to those of you who intend to enlist the aid of a friend or fellow psychic.

EXERCISE NO. 1

For this first exercise, you will need a piece of cloth to serve as a blindfold, and a book. Instruct your partner to place the blindfold over your eyes, then tell him to conceal the book in another room of your home. Of course, you must not be aware of where the book has been hidden nor should your partner allow you any clues.

Once the book is well concealed, say to your partner: "Take my hand and stand beside me. Concentrate your thoughts on the location of the book. Try to think of nothing else. Picture the hiding place in your mind."

Focus your attention on the tingling sensation in your hand. Feel the mental electricity being transferred from your partner's body into your own.

After a few seconds, your friend's thoughts will begin registering in your mind and you will automatically know the proper direction in which to move, whether it be foreward, to the left or to the right. Take three steps in the chosen direction when you are sure of yourself.

Blank your mind again, then let your partner's thought impulses reenter your brain. A new set of directions will register in a few seconds, telling you which way to move. Advance another three steps.

Continue this procedure until certain that you are close to the concealed article. Stop, clear your mind, then tune in on the new thought impulses being transmitted by your partner. An exact image of the hiding place will slowly form in your mind's eye. For example, if the book is hidden in a closet, you will visualize that closet; if it is hidden beneath a chair cushion, you will be able to envision that piece of furniture.

Remove the blindfold, reach down with your free hand and retrieve the book from its hiding place. Provided you followed all directions, the book should be exactly where you envisioned it.

If you didn't succeed in this test, it could be that you merely require further practice. Frequently, a person will fail to correctly interpret his partner's thoughts principally because he is not accustomed to using contact telepathy. If this happens to be true in your case, practice will enable you to tune into another person's mental instructions with greater clarity. Once you are acquainted with this form of communication, you will be able to locate hidden objects in a few seconds with minimal effort.

Take turns performing this exercise with your partner. Each of you should practice this step at least three times so that you will become thoroughly familiar with the basic operation of contact telepathy. For best results, of course, your fellow student should be proficient at perfect relaxation; otherwise, there is little chance of real psychic development occurring.

When you feel that you have mastered this step, proceed to the next exercise.

EXERCISE NO. 2

In this growth lesson, you will learn to perceive thought impulses with maximum clarity. In other words, you'll discover a useful technique for tuning in telepathically for clearer reception.

Instruct your partner to select a set of ten numbers at random, ranging between one and seven. The numbers should be recorded on paper in a vertical column, without you seeing the correct sequence.

Once this is done, clasp your partner's left hand with your right hand. Tell your friend to concentrate intensely on the first number that appears on his list. You must use contact telepathy to dertermine which number is the correct one.

Remember, allow your friend's thought impulses to enter your body. Wait for them to register in your mind, then see what image forms. When you think you have the correct answer, say the number out loud. Using his free hand, your partner should write your answer beside the correct one, then proceed to the second number on his list, continuing in this manner until all ten digits have been transmitted.

When the run is completed, break physical contact and count your correct answers. Use this chart to evaluate your progress.

0-3	— Poor reception
4	— Fair reception
5	— Good reception
6-7	— Very good reception
8 or more	— Excellent reception

Now administer this test to your partner and see how well he scores.

Remember, in this as well as all other growth exercises, the key to telepathic power is practice. If your score is low on the first trial run, it does not mean that you lack psychic potential; merely that you need additional practice.

Repeat this step several times more and your score will increase significantly. If it doesn't, you had better practice perfect relaxation again, working slowly and carefully.

When your score on this test consistently remains above six, you are ready to proceed to the third growth exercise below.

EXERCISE NO. 3

This step is considerably more difficult than the earlier ones. Retire to a quiet, cool room in your home where you will be free from all disturbance. Have your partner select one of the symbols from the following: circle, square, cross, triangle, star.

Then have him form a clear image of the design in his mind's eye. Now place a hand upon your partner's shoulder for approximately fif-

teen seconds. Since your mind is—or should be
—more sensitive to thought impulses, the correct symbol should register in your brain in this
brief span of time. Remove your hand and state
which design you perceived. Keep track of your
answers and, at the end of ten tries, stop and
evaluate your score. Then administer the same
test to your partner.

To chart your progress, refer to the scoring
table for Exercise No. 2.

It is quite probable that the fifteen second
time limit will interfere with your accuracy.
Many people find it difficult to operate under
this kind of pressure. But it is important to remember that when you use touch telepathy in
daily living, you may not be able to maintain
physical contact with a person for more than a
few seconds. For this reason, it is essential that
you learn to work quickly, yet maintain absolute accuracy.

With practice, you will get the knack of this
exercise, so repeat the above test several times
more. Do not proceed until your score remains
consistently above six.

EXERCISE NO. 4

Have your partner select a symbol from
the list given in Exercise No. 3 and follow
the same procedure as outlined above.
But this time, do not place your hand on
your partner's shoulder. Instead, shake
hands for about three seconds, just as you
would do upon meeting a new acquaintance. Your task is to receive and correctly
interpret the symbol being sent to you.
Keep tabs on your score as usual, and practice this step until you master it

EXERCISE NO. 5

Now try this final test: Have your partner select another symbol from the preceeding list and then form a picture of the design in his mind. This time, however, don't clasp hands even briefly. Instead, simply brush against your friend's arm, just as you would do if you had made accidental contact with someone in a crowd. It is up to you to correctly perceive the symbol being transmitted to you.

Practice this last exercise until you are proficient at receiving thoughts through contact telepathy in less than a few seconds.

You should now be adept in the use of touch telepathy. Having mastered the above exercises you are now ready to begin using this unique power in your daily life. You have seen how this form of mental communication works, and already you have experimented with it under a series of conditions.

Contact telepathy can be used in many ways. It is up to you to decide when and how to employ this power. Already you may have devised several practical applications and as time passes you'll probably devise more. But, by all means, be discreet: Never try to use touch telepathy as a weapon against your friends and rivals or you may be the loser in the end.

Also, remember that the power you now possess must be exercised constantly if you want to maintain your present level of development. If you allow your new-found psychic power to stagnate, it will become weak and ineffectual. Use it at every opportunity: with friends, loved ones and contemporaries. Practice several times a week with a fellow student if possible.

ADVANCED TECHNIQUES
OF MIND READING

When you have mastered touch telepathy, you will be ready to unlock another of your hidden psychic powers. This second faculty, mental telepathy, may be developed easily in a matter of a few days. It is similar to contact telepathy in principle, but, if properly applied, it will prove even more useful.

As you may suspect, contact telepathy, while a valuable tool, has limitations. One serious drawback is that you must actually touch a person in order to perceive his thoughts. Quite predictably, there will be occasions when a brief handshake or an "accidental" brush against someone's shoulder might not be possible, especially if you wish to avoid looking suspicious. The value of touch telepathy then goes out the window.

Obviously, your newly acquired power is not effective one hundred percent of the time. And this is where mental telepathy enters the picture. The latter faculty allows you greater versatility, as physical contact is not necessary. In short, it enables you to read someone's mind without having to touch the person.

In an earlier part of this chapter, you learned how the brain generates thought impulses and that this mental electricity saturates the body. By means of contact telepathy, a portion of this energy may be absorbed into your own physical being. This is what happens in thought transference.

Something you did *not* learn before is that thought impulses not only saturate an individual's body but also permeate the surrounding atmosphere. By mentally tuning in and drawing this invisible energy into your brain, the same result is achieved: thought transference.

At first glance, mental telepathy may seem significantly more difficult than touch telepathy, but it actually isn't. In fact, you should be able to master this unique power in just a few days. Since your brain is already sensitized, psychically speaking, and since you are already acquainted with an elementary type of mind-to-mind communication, this new faculty will blossom almost spontaneously.

FIVE HELPFUL HINTS
FOR USING MENTAL TELEPATHY

Below are five hints that will enable you to use the power of mental telepathy to best advantage. Follow these suggestions and you will encounter no difficulty in unlocking this amazing psychic faculty.

1) Whenever you attempt to perceive someone's thoughts, remain calm and at ease. Be confident but not too eager. Anxiety, tension and impatience may impede telepathic reception.

2) Never strain or force your mind into a receptive state. Sensitivity, as mentioned before, comes with practice and in no other way. Over-exertion tends to hinder thought transference and could result in serious side effects. Headache, cramped muscles and nausea are common symptoms of strain. Should one or more of these warning signals develop, take a break and recover. To avoid such adverse conditions, always use perfect relaxation before practicing mental telepathy.

3) Your emotional state has considerable influence on telepathic receptivity. Therefore, never use mind reading when you are angry,

frustrated or depressed. You will probably fail to achieve meaningful results and could compound your original problem. Poor health also tends to interfere with clear reception. For best results, remember that a healthy body and tranquil mind are important for successful telepathy.

4) Try to catch the person's eye and, if possible, lock gazes for a few seconds. You will find that by doing this, thought impulses register in your mind with amazing clarity. The ancient Babylonians believed that the eyes are the secret mirror of the mind. You can prove the validity of this statement to yourself by following this suggestion.

5) This final hint is especially important: When you want to perceive someone's thoughts, hold an image of that person's face in your mind and concentrate on it for approximately fifteen seconds. This process, known as visualization, helps to attract the person's thought impulses into your own mind when physical contact is not possible. Visualization also strengthens weak impulses and promotes added clarity.

VISUALIZATION EXERCISES

It requires no more than a few minutes to master the technique of visualization, time well spent considering the value of this mental secret. What follows is a simple exercise to help familiarize you with the process. Practice it several times so that you will be able to perform visualization quickly and easily.

Obtain a good color photograph of a friend or a relative and retire to a quiet room. Gaze intently at the face in the photo for approximately one minute. Use perfect relaxation to blank all other thoughts from your mind. Concentrate solely on the picture.

At the end of the prescribed time, close your eyes. A clear image of the person's face will appear in your mind, and it will remain there as long as you maintain concentration. This is exactly what should happen in genuine visualization: First, blank your mind, then get a clear mental image of the person's face.

Practice this step once more.

To make certain that you have mastered the technique, here is another exercise slightly more difficult than the first:

Concentrate on the face in the photograph for approximately five seconds. This brief amount of time is not enough to burn a clear image in your mind, but it does allow sufficient time to memorize basic facial features. Now, with your eyes closed, try to formulate and maintain the desired mental image. With practice, you will become competent in the speedy application of the technique.

The ability to perform visualization in a few seconds is of particular importance since you cannot go about staring at people without raising suspicion. An ideal way to practice the technique is to go out in public and gaze at a stranger's face for about five seconds, then attempt to construct a mental image of that person. This can be performed conveniently at work, at school or while casually walking down a street in your city. Also, you can practice when among friends and relatives.

Through great use, you will gradually cultivate this talent. Soon you'll be able to visualize with your eyes wide open. The power of mental telepathy may then be utilized to the fullest extent without anyone so much as suspecting it!

LONG-DISTANCE TELEPATHY

There is a third telepathic power which involves mind-to-mind communication with faraway friends. This unique faculty, distance telepathy, enables you to tune in and receive thought impulses from people who may be hundreds or thousands of miles away at the time. Since this hidden psychic power is normally used in conjunction with another faculty, clairvoyance, for simplicity's sake it is discussed in the next chapter, "Clairvoyance: Your Psychic Television."

A SPECIAL WORD
ABOUT THE USE OF TELEPATHY

Many beginners, in their enthusiasm, understandably try to use mind reading on everyone in sight. This fact is regrettable. Always remember that if you apply good judgment and discretion, telepathy will work to your advantage, making life more rewarding and enjoyable. But if you fail to observe the dictates of common sense, your new power could easily be the source of mental and emotional anguish.

Mind reading must never be used as a means of spying on people or to snoop into their private affairs. More than one person has sacrificed friends, reputation and popularity by using telepathy as a weapon for selfish aims. To a limited extent, prying is a harmless gesture, but when it is carried to extremes it becomes offensive. In the end you will gain nothing but the contempt of your peers.

Most of you who are reading this book are

probably intelligent, constructive people. But there are always a few who try to corrupt all that is within their reach. True enough, telepathy can be used in a selfish or destructive way, but the main purpose of this power is to help you realize better relationships and a deeper, more meaningful form of communication.

The prudent approach to using mental telepathy is to observe the oft-quoted Golden Rule —"Do unto others as you would have them do unto you." Before you read someone's mind, put yourself in their position and ask: "Would I resent this kind of intrusion?" If the answer is yes, get your information in some other way.

One final word to the wise: You may, from time to time, encounter a man or a woman who seems immune to mind reading. With such a person, you will be unable to perceive any thought impulses, even through contact telepathy. If you get the feeling that the individual is enveloped in an invisible protective wall, don't try to force mental communication, for there is a good reason behind this peculiar condition.

It goes without saying that many thousands of people like yourself are learning to use their hidden psychic powers in daily living. But there are some men and women who have been using ESP for years. They have learned to construct an invisible barrier of energy around themselves so that it is impossible to read their minds without their consent. This is purely a matter of self-defense. You, too, will learn how to protect yourself from telepathic intrusion in Chapter Nine, and you will discover a method of psychically repelling those people who attempt to force their way into your mind.

But, for the time being, suffice it to say that

should you encounter an advanced psychic whose mind appears to be blank, do not be disturbed. Such an individual *is* producing thought impulses just like everyone else. The difference is that he has learned to control his flow of mental electricity.

INDICATIONS OF
YOUR PSYCHIC GROWTH

As the days turn into weeks and you grow more accustomed to using telepathic power, a host of benefits will begin to accumulate. Friendships will take on new meaning, love relations will blossom. You may acquire a deeper understanding of human nature, as the needs and secret desires of your friends, your loved ones and contemporaries become more obvious.

Indications of your psychic growth will be manifest in various ways. One day, you may find yourself automatically receiving surface thoughts from total strangers while shopping for groceries or simply walking down a street. Or you might hear a new acquaintance thinking —"My God, you really remind me of so-and-so!"

From that time on, telepathy will play an important role in your daily life.

Chapter Two

Clairvoyance:
The Miracle of Psychic Television

Assuming that you have read and applied the guidelines in the preceding chapter, you should now be adept at receiving thoughts from other people. Chances are, you have already used mind reading on several occasions and seen how this amazing power can add a new dimension to your life.

Telepathy, however, is just one of several hidden psychic powers you possess. It is entertaining and definitely useful, but it is by no means the most spectacular extrasensory gift.

As you will discover in this chapter, the power of clairvoyance, your second major faculty, is even more fascinating and rewarding than mental communication.

Envision the following scene: You are glancing through an old school annual and recall several of your close chums. There is one person whom you would particularly like to meet again, but you have not heard from him for years and have no way to get in touch. Again, you close your eyes and suddenly you can see your long-lost friend's home. You scan the neighborhood surrounding his house, take note of a few street markers and store-front signs. Then, amazingly enough, you know exactly which city to look in. A week later, this eerie vision becomes reality when you find the person's name in the appropriate phone directory and subsequently write or call!

This is an example of clairvoyance, the miracle of psychic television; you can use the power to tune in on distant people and places as well as to see events as they unfold, just as though an invisible TV screen was planted in your mind.

You don't believe it?

If not, your reaction is understandable. Most people find it difficult to believe that clairvoyance really works until they have experienced the incredible phenomenon for themselves. Once they have seen a distant event and later confirmed it, the proof cannot be denied.

In the following pages, the miracle of psychic television will be revealed and you will learn how to refine this extrasensory faculty so that you can use it at will in daily life.

You'll probably find that it is easier to master clairvoyance than it was to refine the power of telepathy. One reason is that you have already learned perfect relaxation, a major factor in the successful use of this new faculty. Another reason is that your mind has been disciplined and sensitized through the practice exercises given in Chapter One. Consequently, you need only master several simple techniques in order to have psychic television at your fingertips.

CLAIRVOYANCE DEFINED

Clairvoyance is a word of French origin, which, literally translated, means to see clearly. Psychically speaking, it means seeing at a distance what the naked eye cannot perceive. This particular faculty is sometimes called psychic vision, distant vision, distance perception and second sight. It may be consciously developed through a series of growth exercises, and its use entails no physical or emotional danger whatsoever.

Similarly to other psychic phenomena, clairvoyance frequently occurs without conscious effort; that is to say, spontaneously. There are frequent reports of psychic vision occurring in times of crisis, especially when a close friend or loved one is in grave physical danger. In such instances, intense emotions seém to trigger second sight.

Clairvoyant experiences frequently occur spontaneously during sleep, but it is often difficult to distinguish the validity of the phenomenon at this time, for there is a tendency to forget such incidents upon waking, or to confuse them with subconscious dream activity.

Generally speaking, clairvoyant power is of five types:

1) Standard "psychic vision," the ability to perceive people, places and events at a distance.

2) Penetrative clairvoyance, also called X-ray vision, which involves mentally seeing through walls and other material barriers.

3) Clairvoyant psychometry, the ability to

psychically locate missing persons and lost or stolen articles.

4) Precognitive clairvoyance, which entails seeing into the future, a power discussed in a later chapter exclusively devoted to accurate prediction.

5) Retro-clairvoyance, the ability to see events of the distant past. This is not to be confused with retrocognition, which is frequently used to recall past life experiences from hundreds of thousands of years ago, and will be discussed at length in a later chapter on reincarnation.

There is a sixth power called clairaudience, a function of particular value. It is distinctly different from the above faculties, for it involves two psychic powers, clairvoyance and telepathy, used conjointly. Clairaudience makes it possible for one to see *and* hear at a distance.

WHAT CLAIRVOYANCE CAN DO FOR YOU

Why should you take the time to unlock the power of clairvoyance?

Clearly, there are a multitude of practical applications for this unique form of ESP. The overall benefits which you derive from clairvoyance depend largely on your personal needs and desires. If your life has thus far been turbulent and emotional gratification is uppermost in your mind, you would probably use this faculty in a different way than the person interested in, say, career advancement. But whether your concern be love, money, friendship or some other personal matter, clairvoyant power can fulfill a variety of needs and add an efficacious new dimension to your life.

Suffice it to say, space does not permit listing

every possible application, but here is just one common example of how this hidden psychic power has proven valuable:

MISSING FRIEND LOCATED

Using psychic vision, I was able to locate Robert N., a close friend of mine who had mysteriously disappeared in the spring of 1970. Over the months, I had often wondered where he was living, but none of our mutual acquaintances had information on his whereabouts.

The same winter, I received a letter from one of Robert's relatives in New York explaining that his mother had been striken by cancer and was not expected to live.

Through the power of clairvoyance, I located my friend in a small rural area of northern Florida, where he had gone after a painful divorce procedure in California. Happily, he was reunited with his mother in her final days.

THE MIRACLE OF PSYCHIC TELEVISION

If you understand the fundamentals of mind-to-mind communication, you should be able to master clairvoyance with no difficulty, as both powers function in accordance with the same basic principles. Rather than hearing thought impulses emanating from other people, however, this second ESP faculty involves psychically tuning in and seeing distant people, places and things.

This explains why clairvoyance is so often equated with the term psychic television. By mastering a few simple techniques, you can observe friends—and total strangers—in action as they carry out their daily affairs, no matter where in the world they may be. You will be able to locate lost or stolen articles and missing persons. You will be able to tune in on distant events as they unfold.

No one knows exactly how clairvoyance works. It has been tested and investigated under strict laboratory controls, and numerous theories have been advanced, yet it remains an enigma. However, it is not necessary to understand the phenomenon in order to cultivate clairvoyant power. The power is real and its efficacious value can be proven through your own experiences.

Clairvoyance has been used advantageously by thousands of people in all departments of life. This unique power can also work for you.

EXPERIMENT

You may be inclined to think that clairvoyance is a complicated function, too difficult and time-consuming for you to master. If so, perform this convincing experiment and prove to your own satisfaction the value and simplicity of this hidden psychic power.

Retire to a quiet room in your house where you will not be disturbed by noise or other distractions. You should have with you a color photograph of a close friend or relative, preferably someone who resides in another city or state. Use perfect relaxation to subdue your mind and body, then concentrate on the face in the photo for ten or fifteen seconds, just to get reacquainted with the person's basic features.

Now perform visualization, using the easy techniques given in the preceding chapter. When the desired image registers clearly in your mind's eye, hold it there for approximately thirty seconds. Then, simply relax and watch what happens. Do not attempt to receive or send thoughts. Do absolutely nothing except observe what happens to the mental picture.

Gradually, your friend's face will appear to take on a life-like quality. You may notice a change of expression or some other facial gesture such as an eye movement. As you continue to watch, the original image may become fuzzy and practically fade out, but a few moments later, a surprising thing will occur: You should be able to see your friend actually moving around in an entirely new setting, vaguely at first, but with ever-increasing clarity. He or she may be walking down a street, strolling through a park, working in an office or doing any number of things. Although you will hear no sound whatsoever, the details of this extrasensory vision should be amazingly clear.

You will find that you can maintain this live image and observe your friend's activities on psychic television for as long as you desire. When you tire of watching, or if headache or nausea should develop due to mental fatigue, simply open your eyes and the uncanny experience will end.

What has occurred? You have just undergone a genuine clairvoyant experience. You tuned in on your friend and observed his every action at the same moment it was happening. Your reception might not have been consistently clear, but, on your first attempt, that is to be expected. With practice, you can refine this faculty to the highest point of efficiency and receive clear, vivid impressions with minimal time and effort!

If you are already convinced that clairvoyance is a genuine phenomenon, merely practice this exercise, tuning in on several different people so that you will derive maximum benefit from the step.

If you remain a disbeliever, there is a way you can verify the accuracy of this experiment to your own satisfaction. First, record every detail that you perceived, as well as the date and time of the experience. Then write a brief note to the man or woman who unknowingly participated in the test, asking what the person was doing at the exact moment you tuned in. Be sure to mail the letter promptly so that your friend's memory will still be sharp when he receives it.

In a week to ten days you should get a reply. Don't be surprised if it corresponds perfectly with the impressions you percieved on your psychic television!

HOW TO CULTIVATE THE POWER OF PSYCHIC VISION

It has been clearly established through the above experiment that almost everyone possesses latent clairvoyant abilities. You may be surprised to know that refining this unique ESP faculty is an easy matter, provided you observe several sensible guidelines.

First, you must master the special visualization technique presented in the preceding step, then practice until you become proficient in its use. This particular process is essential to the successful operation of your psychic television. If you cannot visualize, you can't expect to receive meaningful impressions, just as you cannot make a regular TV set function without a working picture tube.

Second, you must cultivate mental discipline. It is vitally important that you maintain perfect control of your mind and body during clairvoyant experiences. No stray thoughts should be allowed to enter your mind; otherwise, the clarity of your reception will be affected and a jumbled maze of unintelligible impressions could result. Although you learned self-discipline to some extent in Chapter One, it must now be further refined.

Lastly, your power of concentration requires additional improvement. What you learned in the previous chapter on mind-to-mind communication is not quite enough. Clairvoyance requires greater concentration than mind reading, principally because you are not merely trying to perceive a nearby person's thoughts, but trying to reach out and physically see with vivid clarity, what is happening over a distance of hundreds or thousands of miles. To do this, you must develop: ultra-concentration.

Appearing below is a proven, step-by-step procedure designed to help you refine the three above-mentioned qualities in the briefest possible time. Once you master these techniques, your psychic television will be fully operative and you'll be able to use the power of clairvoyance whenever desired.

Proceed with confidence, but avoid going to extremes. Restricting your progress through over-caution can be as detrimental to the process of individual psychic growth as forging recklessly ahead without the benefit of adequate preparation or training. Therefore, determine a speed which is personally suitable and move from one step to the next only when you feel that you are ready to do so.

This systematic approach, recommended for its basic simplicity, insures safe and complete development of your clairvoyant power. But you must use common sense. If unsure of your performance in a particular step, simply practice until you are satisfied. Remember, it is better to invest extra time and energy than to sacrifice your previous achievements by taking shortcuts.

STEP NO. 1

This step should be practiced for five consecutive days without fail, preferably during the late evening hours, a time when relative tranquility prevails. If by chance your nights are occupied, the early hours of the morning will suffice.

Situate yourself in a comfortable chair, facing approximately ten feet away from a plain white wall in your home. Use perfect relaxation to subdue your mind and body.

Find a small crack in the paint, a nail hole or some other point upon which you can focus your attention. If desired, a small ink dot located at eye level and drawn beforehand will fulfill the requirement.

Gaze intently at the specified marking. Focus your full attention on that spot and, if perchance your concentration falters, gently expel any intruding thought or sensation from your mind and redirect your attention toward the wall. No matter what happens, however, do not permit any interruption to distract you.

Maintain your concentration for approximately three minutes, then close your eyes for a few seconds and rest before resuming your normal activities.

PROGRESS TEST

Upon completing the fifth day of Step One, your power of concentration should be operating at peak efficiency and your mind should be trained to perceive minute detail, an important component of distant visualization.

But how can you honestly know if you are ready to go on to the next step?

To eliminate the guesswork, a simple progress test has been prepared for your convenience. Merely answer the following questions "yes" or "no." (If your answer is "sometimes," mark "yes.")

1) While performing Step One, do you experience restlessness?

2) Does your mind have a tendency to wander?

3) Is it difficult for you to concentrate in the prescribed manner for three full minutes?

4) Do you experience:
   a) Cramped muscles?
   b) Nausea?
   c) Chronic headache?
   d) Other discomfort?

5) Does noise, movement or other commotion interrupt your concentration?

6) Do you believe you need further practice?

7) Have you failed to practice Step One on any of the five designated days?

To determine your score, add up your number of "yes" answers and consult the following table for your rating and instructions:

IF YOUR SCORE IS 0: Perfect! You can rest assured that you have learned this phase to the tee. Proceed to Step Two at once.

IF YOUR SCORE IS 1-2: You are experiencing a few minor difficulties and another day of practice would not hurt. However, you are ready to go on to the next step. Try not to force yourself and you'll most likely encounter better results.

IF YOUR SCORE IS 3: You haven't quite mastered Step One. Two or three days of practice is suggested, then proceed to Step Two.

IF YOUR SCORE IS 4 OR MORE: You certainly missed the point of the preceding exercise. It could be that you are trying too hard or need work in the area of perfect relaxation. See Chapter One and repeat this step before continuing. This score does not reflect a lack of psychic potential, but merely shows that you cannot relax well enough to develop ultra-concentration.

Incidentally, if you answered "yes" to Questions 4a-4d, you are advised to review the art of perfect relaxation, regardless of your overall score on this test. Cramped muscles, headache, nausea and other physical discomforts symptomize tension and mental stress. Such adverse conditions should never occur: Besides being downright unpleasant, this could easily hinder the exercise of your hidden psychic power.

How well did you score on the test? If you passed, the difficult part is over and you are well on your way to benefiting from the power of clairvoyance.

STEP NO. 2

This next step is not only easier than the first one, but more enjoyable as well.

Obtain a magazine with color photographs, such as those used in full-page advertisements. Skim through from cover to cover until you locate a photo of a man or woman whose face intrigues you.

Try to visualize the person's face in your mind, using the same technique you learned in the experiment at the beginning of this chapter and summarized here for your convenience:

a) Achieve perfect relaxation.
b) Gaze intently at the picture: Use ultra-concentration for best results.
c) Close your eyes and project an exact image of the face onto the screen of your psychic television.
d) Maintain the image for thirty seconds, then relax and watch what happens.

Gradually, the face will come to life with a slight gesture or a change of expression. Soon afterwards, the image will begin to melt away, but a moment later an entire scene will unfold. You will actually be able to see the person carrying out his or her daily affairs.

If you performed this step correctly, your subject's location should not matter: He or she may be thousands of miles away, but the image appearing on your psychic television should be clear and vivid.

As you can see, you do not need to know a person in order to tune in through psychic television. In fact, some people claim that it is easier to focus on strangers than friends, although there is no real reason for this feeling: Psychic television should function equally well in either case. Of course, it may be virtually impossible to verify the accuracy of impressions received in the above experiment, but this is nevertheless an excellent opportunity for practice in visualizing.

For additional practice, try tuning in on several other strangers using the same technique, until you are thoroughly acquainted with its operation. Then go on to the final step.

STEP NO. 3
To complete this last step, go to a park or other public place where you will find people relaxing. Situate yourself several hundred feet away from someone, but do not be too conspicuous. Use perfect relaxation to blank your mind, then gaze intently at your chosen subject for a few seconds.

Now close your eyes and try to visualize. If your subject is seated on a park bench, for example, envision exactly that with absolute clarity. Project the image onto your psychic television screen, hold it for about one minute, then blank your mind again and relax.

While this exercise is by no means as spectacular as the preceding one, it does provide a final opportunity for supervised practice and to refine any serious flaws in your technique. Therefore, perform the step two or three times, visualizing a different stranger on each occasion so as to be absolutely certain that you have fully developed your psychic vision.

HOW TO TUNE IN
ON FRIENDS AND STRANGERS
Through the miracle of psychic television, you can tune in on friends and strangers across the world with practically no effort. All you need is a sharp, color photograph of the person you wish to see and the knowledge contained in the above three-step program. If a photo cannot be obtained, you should at least have a general idea of the individual's facial appearance.

Follow the simple instructions outlined in Step No. 2 and within minutes your psychic television will be lit up by vivid colorful scenes. You can watch an entire drama unfold, then open your eyes and the image automatically vanishes with no aftereffects. Close your eyes again and you can tune in on someone else just as easily. In the space of a single hour, you can focus on five, six, seven or more people. It's that easy.

All that remains now is for you to apply this new knowledge and use your psychic television in daily living.

Chapter Three

Advanced Secrets of Clairvoyance

The miracle of psychic television, revealed in Chapter Two, is probably the most important feature of clairvoyance, but it is by no means the sole characteristic of this unique extrasensory talent.

There are three other distinct variations of second sight which have not yet been examined: clairaudience, penetrating clairvoyance and psychometric clairvoyance. The first adds a new dimension to psychic television, for it enables you to see *and* hear at a distance. The second variation, penetrating clairvoyance, is not as important as the others; also called X-ray vision, it is used to physically see through walls, locked containers and like material barriers.

The talent of psychometric clairvoyance is especially valuable. It enables you to locate lost or stolen objects, as well as missing persons. It is not only efficacious in personal matters but is an effective weapon against crime. Renowned seers who are called upon by law enforcement agencies to locate escaped criminals or lost children and to solve various types of crime traditionally use psychometric clairvoyance to obtain revealing information.

Each of these amazing powers can be easily developed in a few hours or a day at the most. Since all function in much the same way as psychic vision, which was previously discussed at length, you need only familiarize yourself with several elementary techniques.

Here are just two examples, taken from real life, illustrating how the abilities now under discussion have proven worthwhile:

SOS TRAVELS 1,000 MILES

During the summer of 1972, Todd and Carol M., a married couple I had known for several years, left Los Angeles for a camping trip in northern Oregon. I had agreed to care for their Persian cat while they were away, and Todd provided me with an uncle's phone number where they would be staying part of the time and could be reached in case of an emergency.

Several days later, I was at home reading when I received a telepathic distress signal from Carol. The SOS was extremely weak, probably because it was being transmitted subconsciously. I immediately telephoned Todd's uncle, but the relative informed me that my two friends had not yet arrived at his house.

Through the miracle of psychic television, I determined that the couple were trapped in a mountainous area, which was impossible to pinpoint on terrestial features. But clairaudience permitted me to *hear* them talking and it was not long before I discovered that they were in Oregon, about ten miles northwest of their relative's home.

I called the uncle again, and after convincing him that I was quite serious, explained what I had perceived. Finally, he agreed to locate and search the area I described.

Later the same night, Todd and Carol were safe from their ordeal.

CHILD'S DISAPPEARANCE SOLVED

In February, 1972, I was contacted by a distraught mother who had attended one of my lectures on parapsychology. She explained that, following an argument, her thirteen year old daughter had run away from home, and asked for my assistance in locating her.

I consented and asked for a color photograph of the missing girl, but I was dismayed to learn that the only pictures of her in existence were taken when she was an infant, therefore useless for tuning in via psychic television.

Fortunately, I was acquainted with the power of psychometric clairvoyance. Through this faculty, I managed to locate the girl at a friend's house nearby. I accompanied the mother to the location I had perceived and the two feuding relatives made their peace.

HOW TO RECEIVE SOUNDS THROUGH SPACE

Until now, you have been able to see people on psychic television, but no sounds register in your mind, even though someone's mouth seems to be moving. Since you are most likely not a professional lip-reader, you should develop

59

clairaudience: This extra-sensory ability will enable you to *hear* what people say as well as see them on your psychic television screen.

To cultivate this talent, you need only train your mind to perceive minute sound vibrations. This can be accomplished in a suprisingly easy way. Just practice the following exercises and the power of clairaudience will gradually develop, becoming fully operative in approximately one week, depending on the amount of time you spend practicing.

These growth steps should be performed at night just before you fall asleep. Lie down, close your eyes, relax and follow instructions:

1) Listen to the sound of a dripping faucet in another part of your home. If none of your faucets leak, adjust one to trickle lightly beforehand. Concentrate on nothing but this sound for three minutes.

2) Place a wristwatch on a stand near your bed and try to hear it ticking. Force your mind to tune in on this sound, then mentally amplify it as though the watch had been placed right next to your ear. Then, concentrate on nothing but this ticking for three minutes.

3) Concentrate on the drone of automobiles on a distant street or highway. Try to single out one car and attune your mind to the sound it makes for about a minute. Repeat the exercise several times so that you can perform it without difficulty.

4) When the above steps have been successfully completed, tune in on someone via psychic television. If the person you selected is alone and passive, focus on someone else whose lips are moving. You should now be able to perceive faint sounds, similar to whispering. Con-

centrate your full attention on the voice and try to amplify it. With practice, volume and clarity will develop. Each time you hear someone speaking on psychic television in the future, the person's speech will be more audible.

HOW TO USE X-RAY VISION

If you have practiced the steps in the preceding chapter, you should have no trouble cultivating the next talent. Penetrative clairvoyance, or X-ray vision, the ability to mentally see through walls and like obstructions, is virtually identical to the power of psychic vision, and most of the principles involved have already been revealed. In both cases, a special process known as visualization is used. This, in turn, actuates the miracle of psychic television.

The sole difference between the two powers is that penetrative clairvoyance enlists a slightly different method of visualizing. Rather than facilitating perception at a distance, this new technique permits you to mentally see beyond physical barriers such as walls and into locked containers.

You should be able to cultivate the power of X-ray vision in less than a day. Simply practice the following exercise until you are acquainted with the procedure. Be sure to observe all instructions for best results. Then devise several of your own exercises and apply the same guidelines.

To begin with, two items are necessary: a deck of regular playing cards, and a small metal or wooden box with a lid. Select a particular suit at random and remove those cards. For example, if you choose hearts, separate all thirteen from the deck and place the remainder aside.

Shuffle the cards that you will be working with, then place them in a stack face down on the table before you. Without looking, drop the first card into the box and close the lid. Follow these steps for unlocking the power of X-ray vision:

1) Blank your mind through perfect relaxation.

2) Gaze intently at the sealed container for approximately one minute. Use ultra-concentration to burn an exact image of the box in your mind.

3) Close your eyes and perform standard visualization.

4) Mentally envision that a hole is being burned in the side of the container. Imagine the metal melting away (or if wood, burning) until a sizeable opening appears. If necessary, repeat this step until the desired result is obtained.

5) Now use the miracle of psychic television to look through the hole and see the card at the base of the container. Determine which number appears on the face of the card, then relax and recover.

6) Open the lid and see if you were correct. It might be wise to have pencil and paper handy so that you can record your score.

7) Repeat the entire procedure until you can consistently determine the correct number on each card, or until satisfied with your progress.

Whenever you find it necessary to use the

power of penetrative clairvoyance, simply observe the steps outlined above. Work slowly and carefully, but never strain: X-ray vision should occur naturally, not by force. Most important, be patient and have faith in your own abilities.

THE SECRET OF PSYCHOMETRIC CLAIRVOYANCE

As explained earlier in this chapter, psychometric clairvoyance has two separate functions: It can be used to locate missing people and to recover lost or stolen objects when all conventional means are exhausted. This particular ESP faculty may be developed quickly and with relative ease, in spite of the fact that it is perhaps the most advanced form of clairvoyant power.

Unlike most variations of second sight, which require that you have a photograph of someone in order to tune in on the person, psychometric clairvoyance is more versatile. It can be used effectively in conjunction with the miracle of psychic television to locate any man, woman or child. No photograph is required. In fact, it is not even necessary to know what the individual looks like. Hence, through this unique extrasensory gift, you can ascertain the whereabouts of a long-lost friend, a relative who has withdrawn into seclusion, a neighbor's missing child or a total stranger.

By the same token, you can use the talent to recover any lost or stolen object no matter what it is or how small it may be: a key, a ring, an article of clothing, a purse or wallet, a radio, television, office machine, even your car.

HOW TO RECOVER LOST OR STOLEN OBJECTS

First: Use perfect concentration to blank your mind, then visualize the missing object with as much detail and clarity as possible. Maintain the mental image for about a minute.

Second: Relax and observe. Allow the picture in your mind to gradually fade away.

Third: A few seconds later, a vivid scene should appear on your psychic television screen depicting the exact location of the object. For example, if the missing article is in your own home, you may see a drawer, a cabinet or some other location. Or if the object is presently out-of-doors, scan the surrounding neighborhood for identifying landmarks such as street markers and names of stores.

Fourth: When you have pinpointed the exact location, you should find the missing object precisely in the place you perceived!

HOW TO LOCATE MISSING PEOPLE

As stated before, psychometric clairvoyance can be used to determine any man or woman's whereabouts without the benefit of a color photograph. However, you *must* have in your possession some object which has been in physical contact with the person you wish to find. This will act as a psychic antenna and will assist you in pinpointing the individual's exact location. Clothing worn recently is ideal, but a ring, a watch or some other object which the person has worn or touched will suffice.

Having satisfied this requirement, proceed as follows:

First: Use perfect relaxation to subdue your mind and body. Then, take the person's garment or other possession into your hands, holding it lightly between the fingers.

Second: Concentrate on the psychic vibrations emanating from this homemade antenna. Let the impulses enter your hands and travel upward to your brain. In a few seconds, a slight dizziness may come over you, but this is no cause for alarm.

Third: Leave your mind open to any images which may be forming. Gradually, a picture will begin to solidify. Within a matter of seconds, you should be able to clearly envision the missing person.

Fourth: Carefully observe the details in the surrounding environment. Scan the neighborhood for street markers and store signs. Billboards and other roadside advertising may sometimes provide helpful clues as to the correct city and state.

Fifth: The information you perceive in this manner should permit you to pinpoint the individual's precise whereabouts.

From this point on, it's up to you. Everything that is presently known about developing the power of clairvoyance has been revealed in this and the preceding chapter. You should now be familiar with the miracle of psychic television, what it is and how it works, and be able to tune in on friends and strangers across the world with great ease. You have learned the secret of X-ray vision, how to locate missing persons and lost or stolen objects, and how to hear voices over vast distances.

No one can tell you when or how to use your powers. That is for you to determine as the need arises in the course of your daily affairs. You may want to use this ESP gift frequently, or you may take advantage of it only in times of emergency. In either case, however, always remember to be discreet and considerate.

In the final analysis, the tremendous advantages at your disposal should prove time and again that the energy invested in your training has been well spent.

Chapter Four

How to Make Accurate Predictions

There is a mysterious unseen province, far removed from this mundane civilization of ours, where time and space do not exist. We call it: the future. It is a dimension that defies logical explanation, an unknown frontier where the secrets of tomorrow are concealed from mortal eyes.

Since the twilight of history, man has cursed this elusive domain, and tried to penetrate its barrier. Yet the future has remained stubbornly unconquerable. Even those enterprising dreamers of the past who contrived the notion of the time machine found that their efforts were in vain. The only known mechanical contraptions of this sort were crudely constructed, and seemingly designed to produce odd whirring noises which hardly brought about the desired result.

Fortune-telling, another means of assaulting the future, originated long before the dawn of recorded history, but the multitude of techniques, oracles and prophetic devices proved no more productive than the legendary time machine. Of all the forms of divination, cartomancy, the ancient art of fortune-telling by cards, is probably the most famous. But, in the final analysis, those who piously consulted the system discovered that cards were better used for poker or rummy.

Ironically, while the majority of the populace consorted with gypsies and wizened sorcerers, seers such as Nostradamus quite inconspicuously used their inborn psychic powers to obtain vivid insights into their own destiny and the future of the world. Nostradamus, in fact, recorded extensive predictions on countless subjects of varying importance and used his hidden mental power to accurately foresee events which would not occur until thousands of years later. More recently, such notables as Jeane Dixon, Doc Anderson and Joseph DeLouise have put their extrasensory gifts to practical use and offerred up prognostications, the majority of which have proven amazingly accurate.

The future can be foreseen, not through the portal of a time machine or by a deck of cards, but rather through the power of ESP. And you may be surprised to know that every man, woman and child alive possesses the ability to make accurate predictions and to chart the course of destiny.

How can you penetrate the time barrier? It's easy, if you know how to use a unique psychic power: precognition.

PRECOGNITION DEFINED

In Latin, the word precognition means "to

know before," and modern parapsychologists abide by this definition. In the study of ESP, we equate precognition with the ability to psychically perceive an activity or event before it happens.

Precognition, like other extrasensory phenomena, may occur spontaneously or as the result of conscious effort. It may be triggered during sleep (prophetic dreams), through deliberate concentration, through emotional stress and trauma, or it may be induced through hypnotic trance.

Various terms are synonymously identified with precognition. Future vision, precognitive vision, intuition, accurate prediction and prophesy are among the most common. In certain parts of Norway and other Scandinavian countries, clairvoyance and second sight are sometimes used to describe the phenomena, but in this particular text, the scope of the latter two terms shall be limited to functions mentioned in Chapters Two and Three.

The terms divination, premonition, hunch, and prediction (as defines a specific instance) are erroneously used interchangeably with precognition. Divination, however, refers to a system or technique of fortune-telling completely apart from the ESP talent under discussion. A hunch connotes a specific incident of intuitive feeling, usually favorable, while a premonition is almost always equated with such adversities as disaster, grave danger or loss.

Prediction is used both to describe the act of making prophecies and to describe a single incident.

Note that the words hunch and premonition are as a general rule equated with intuitive feelings of a highly personal nature, while predictions are more universal. The latter entails making a formal statement that describes a future event of far-reaching importance.

As a rule of thumb, remember that a World War is predicted, and your own personal losses and gains are signalled by a hunch if good, a premonition if adverse.

HYPNOSIS AND PRECOGNITION: A DANGEROUS COMBINATION

Beyond spontaneous phenomena which occur unintentionally and conscious prediction, the gift of precognition can sometimes be activated through hypnosis. In the past decade, parapsychologists have experimented with this technique and obtained varying results. The so-called trance state has been implemented in some instances to regress a man or a woman into the distant past as well as to promote future vision.

It is important to note, however, that the value of hypnosis has been greatly exaggerated by modern writers, while the dangers of this process are virtually ignored. I have had many occasions to observe the use of hypnosis in connection with ESP at close quarters, through the work of other qualified researchers and feel compelled at this point to state that the two are a dangerous combination.

The chief drawback is that the trance state makes one's mind usually sensitive to psychic vibrations, but at the same time the individual forfeits a part of his self-control. Consequently, should tragic or otherwise unsettling images register in the mind, there is a grave danger of emotional and psychological trauma.

As a rule of thumb, never permit a friend—or a professional, for that matter—to hypnotize you with the intent to send you backwards or forwards into time. The risks involved are too great. And there is a safer, more natural way to unlock your precognition which is revealed in this chapter. Master the step-by-step technique, and you will not need hypnosis to see into the future.

WARNING SIGN OR CERTAIN DOOM?

In the years since beginning my career as a psychic, I have been called on many times to use the gift of precognition, in my personal affairs as well as in a broader, more universal sense. I have made prophecies concerning my marriage, career and future, and I have also used the power for the benefit of friends and strangers.

People continually ask: "Is all life predestined, or can fate be consciously altered?"

The issue of destiny vs. free will has been the focal point of intense controversy for years. There are some who cling to the philosophy that what tomorrow holds in store is inevitable, that visions of the future cannot be changed.

I am not one to agree with this trend of thought. I do not believe our lives are mapped out from the moment of birth. If that be true, why bother working for personal improvement or happiness. If fate rules our daily affairs, then no matter what we do, we are merely wasting time. Why tend to our health? If it is in our destiny, no matter how neglectful we may be, we should flourish in old age.

WHAT PRECOGNITION CAN DO FOR YOU

Hopefully, you will know better than to ignore the insights acquired through your gift of precognition. The techniques revealed in the following pages, if properly used, will assist you in unlocking this valuable ESP faculty, or to refine it if you have already experienced hunches and premonitions. Through practice, you should be able to foretell your own or another's destiny with ease.

You can realize a host of extraordinary benefits. You'll be able to foresee impending difficulty and to avoid needless loss when trouble does strike. Likewise, you may gain new insights into the fate of your marriage, friendships, your health and career.

The knowledge contained in this chapter will assist you in foretelling the good and bad that lies ahead. By taking advantage of this advance information, averting potential pitfalls and capitalizing on golden opportunities as they arise, you will have mastered a secret of successful living.

FOUR STEPS TO ACCURATE PREDICITON
How can you unlock the mystery of the future?

An easy-to-understand program, consisting of four steps designed to help you cultivate the gift of precognition in a matter of days, has been included in this chapter for your convenience. The steps are:
1) Evaluating prophetic dreams.
2) Understanding hunches and premonitions.
3) Attaining precognitive awareness.
4) Mastering the secret of precognitive vision (and using it at will).

Once you have become familiar with the simple techniques involved in these steps and have practiced them, you will be well on your way to accurate prediction.

STEP NO. 1: EVALUATING PROPHETIC DREAMS

Generally speaking, there are six headings under which all dreams are classified: physical reactive, emotional post reactive, pre-conductive, psychological trauma, deep symbolic, and prophetic.

What exactly is a "prophetic" dream?

It is *not* a dramatic revelation of the future that suddenly overpowers your senses, as some people may think. It is merely a dream which provides a glimpse into the realm of tomorrow, a vision of the future.

You may not realize it, but your subconscious activities while asleep often focus on some forthcoming event. Many times, such a prophetic experience is ignored, or altogether dismissed from your mind upon awakening. However, if you know how to remember and interpret your dreams, it is possible to acquire amazing insights into the secrets of destiny.

The prophetic dream is characterized by distinct conditions and observations:

a) Drifting in the air at an altitude of about twenty feet and observing an event or action while remaining completely objective.

b) Gazing through a window-like opening and watching an event or series of events unfold as though on television.

c) Hearing a date repeated in your mind, or seeing a date marked on a calendar while a certain incident unfolds.

d) Immediately waking after a vivid

dream and being overpowered by a desire to mention the experience to the person involved. If you yourself were involved, feeling compelled to act immediately on what was perceived.

e) Being convinced that, beyond a doubt, the dream in question was clearly prophetic.

Acting On Prophetic Dreams

Before you can fully understand the significance of a precognitive sleep experience, you must first determine whether the dream was of a personal nature, semi-personal (involving people you know), or impersonal, such as a national or international prediction.

Once this is done, you should be able to interpret the dream with relative ease. Prophetic visions are nearly always lucid in content and in meaning. Hence, what you dream is an exact portrayal of the future.

Remember, however, that fate is not inevitable. A personal dream reflects what will happen *provided you do not intervene*. If the presaged event is unfavorable, you can work to prevent it from becoming reality. If the dream betokens success, you need only remain alert and act for maximum gain when the time is right.

The same is true of semi-personal visions. Tell the person involved what you mentally saw and explain the meaning of prophetic dreams. It then becomes your friend's responsibility to use the information to his best advantage.

How To Cause A Prophetic Dream and See Into the Future

Precognition during sleep is usually spontaneous. However, you can intentionally produce prophetic dreams and so acquire a more specific knowledge of your destiny.

While lying in bed on the verge of sleep, focus your mind on a specific question pertaining to the future. For example, if you want to determine the fate of your marriage, envision a clear image of you and your mate standing together hand in hand. At the same time ask yourself: "What will be the state of our marriage in a month (or year)?"

Repeat the question three or four times in your mind and concentrate on the image for a minute or two. Then go directly to sleep without permitting any other thoughts to interfere.

When you waken the next morning, you may be surprised to discover that you had a dream about the future of your marriage relationship!

In the same way as one can determine the fate of a marriage, *it is also possible to discover the identity of a future love mate.*

Again, while in bed and on the verge of sleep, concentrate on a question. Simply blank your mind through perfect relaxation and ask: "Who shall be my future love?"

Repeat the question over and over until you drift into sleep.

In the morning, you may awaken with a stranger's name on the tip of your tongue, or an accurate impression of your future lover in your mind. If you practice this step, you will even be able to discover where the person lives, his (or her) present occupation, and the time and place where you will meet!

How To Record Your Dreams

It is important that you maintain a complete record of your dreams. Therefore, keep a pen and notebook near your bed and upon waking each day, write down every detail of your dreams that you can recall. This should be done immediately, while the memory is fresh; otherwise, you could easily forget the entire dream.

Pay particular attention to prophetic visions. In this way, you may remain in constant contact with the realm of the future and keep informed of forthcoming events.

STEP NO. 2: UNDERSTANDING HUNCHES AND PREMONITIONS

Dreams, as you have seen, are an important source of information and, if properly understood, they can bestow a tremendous advantage over the future.

Hunches and premonitions are another of man's natural psychic resources. Practically everyone has at some time or another responded to these minute inner stirrings and gained through a lucky hunch or averted disaster by heeding a strong premonition. Businessmen, doctors and even the police have frequently accredited their success to playing a hunch.

What follows is an easy method for refining this amazing form of intuition and amplifying the subtle precognitive feelings you and I receive in the course of our daily affairs.

How To Recognize Hunches

Have you ever experienced an overwhelming sensation of good fortune just prior to embarking on a special, or perhaps risky, undertaking? Have you ever felt just plain lucky at times? Chances are you have.

Many times we tend to ignore subtle feelings which are just as important as the ones which overwhelm us. Important hunches sometimes seem trivial, simply because we are more intuitive on some days than others.

Use these easy-to-remember guidelines in all your daily affairs and you will then be better able to recognize favorable feelings and to act on them as they arise.

First: Consider your position. If an important decision is required, place the matter foremost in your mind and concentrate on nothing else; if speculation is involved, focus your thoughts on the proposal at hand.

Second: Review the alternatives. In making a decision, review every possible avenue at your disposal. Where gambles are concerned, consider all the pros and cons.

Third: Evaluate your response. Ask yourself: "How do I really feel about the problem?" Don't let logic interfere with your intuition. In a few moments, the correct answer will formulate in your mind, accompanied by a lucky or otherwise favorable feeling. If you follow this hunch, no matter how unlikely the outcome may seem at the time, you should never again make a wrong or foolish decision and gains of all kinds will come your way.

How To Recognize Premonitions

A premonition quite simply is a warning of impending disaster. Premonitions may vary in intensity, depending on how intuitive you may be on a particular day. Some may be compelling, others weak, yet in either case the implication is the same: Do not proceed.

Many times, we will receive a mild premonition but ignore it and proceed with our original plans, thinking nothing more of it. Not long afterwards, we encounter resistance and say: "If only I had listened to that premonition . . ." But by then it is too late.

Whenever you are making plans, mulling over a proposition, considering a risky enterprise or any major change, don't ignore these intuitive feelings. If you sense impending loss, scandal or disaster in any degree, immediately alter your plans. You may never know the outcome of your original course of action, but it is better to be safe than sorry.

How To Amplify Hunches and Premonitions

If you consistently observe the above guidelines, you should begin to notice a remarkable improvement in your life. You will make fewer mistakes, avoid loss due to poor judgment and derive countless gains in all undertakings. This form of intuition may assist you in selecting the proper love mate, business associates and friends, as well as provide you with financial, social and other tangible gains.

Through great use, your intuition will become more acute. If you make a habit of following hunches and premonitions, you will soon discover that these feelings occur more frequently and register more vividly in your mind with practically no effort on your part.

Which, of course, is the whole idea of this chapter.

STEP NO. 3: ATTAINING PRECOGNITIVE AWARENESS

Precognitive awareness refers to a specific state of mind in which your intuition is allowed to operate without restraint. Many amateur and professional seers use it to forsee their personal destiny as well as to make predictions of international consequence.

To attain precognitive awareness, you must

become acutely sensitive to intuitive impulses produced by the psychic regions of the brain. Although this may sound complicated, the easy-to-master growth exercise which follows will permit you to achieve the desired sensitivity virtually overnight.

Late in the afternoon or evening, relax in a quiet room of your home. Blank your mind, then use ultra-concentration to burn an actual image of some date in the future into your mind.

Visualize the date in bold letters for approximately five minutes. Think of absolutely nothing but mentally transporting yourself to that point in the future.

After three minutes or so, you may experience slight dizziness, or a ringing in the ears; however, this is perfectly natural and is no cause for alarm. Simply maintain your concentration.

At the conclusion of five minutes, with your eyes still closed, allow the date image to slowly vanish from your mind. For the next few seconds, you will be suspended in a darkened, soundless void. Moments later, however, a strange thing should begin to happen: Although your mind remains completely blank, peculiar feelings will start registering in your brain.

When this happens, turn your thoughts to a prominent personality in present time, such as the President or some actor or actress whom you admire. A strong sensation of optimism or hopelessness should overpower you, indicating your chosen subject's destiny in the year you have selected. In other words, you are intuitively experiencing the fate which awaits that particular person.

Perform the same experiment with other

well-known personalities, or with friends and relatives. Each time, you will find that the same amazing thing happens.

At the end of thirty or forty minutes, conclude the session. Record the exact sensations you experienced in connection with each person's fate. File this information in a safe place, for you may want to verify your accuracy in the years ahead.

Practice this step once or twice a day until precognitive awareness comes naturally.

STEP NO. 4: THE SECRET OF PRECOGNITIVE VISION

You can learn how to actually see into the future. This amazing power will permit you to clearly foresee your own or another person's fate years in advance. Used conjointly with the techniques and natural resources described in the previous three steps, you'll be able to make accurate predictions for yourself, your friends and loved ones, even total strangers. And, if you are so inclined, you may use your newly-acquired powers to foretell the future of the world!

Impossible? Practice and see for yourself: Blank your mind through perfect relaxation. Select a date in the near future and visualize it, using ultra-concentration. At the end of three minutes, let the image gradually fade from your mind. Precognitive awareness should ensue within seconds. Now, instead of striving to keep your mind blank of all images, activate your psychic television. Vivid impressions of the future will automatically begin to register, just as distant people, places and events did when you mastered the techniques outlined in

Chapter Two.

To activate the miracle of psychic television, you need only to leave your mind open and permit images to register. If you have performed the entire experiment correctly, the intuitive feelings you experience should automatically translate into pictures through a subconscious process. These impressions, in turn, are broadcast on psychic television and vivid images of the future unfold.

The same process may be used to tune in on any month or year of the future, simply by visualizing the desired date and following all other instructions.

You now have a power that man has dreamed about for centuries. Use it. With practice, you can become highly adept; as with most things, proficiency comes with experience.

One final word: Always record your predictions on paper. This will enable you to keep track of what you foresee and to verify your accuracy. Further, if you predict major world events, give a written copy of your prophesies to a friend. In this way, you can prove that you honestly foresaw the event in advance.

As the saying goes, anyone can make a prediction—after the event happens. But if you maintain a written record of your prophesies, there will be no room for doubt.

Chapter Five

How To Control Matter With ESP

The concept of mind over matter has intrigued man since the earliest times. Thousands of people in every culture have dreamed about possessing such a power, and a few enterprising scholars of the past have sought ways to unlock and cultivate it.

Psychokinesis, the scientific term for mind over matter, has existed for centuries. The early cave dwellers used it to control the elements. Through their practice of magic and sorcery, which most contemporary authorities agree is merely a sophisticated approach to generating extrasensory power, they were said to have controlled the weather as well as crops and livestock. Medieval occultists and witches used thought energy to control the material realm in much the same way.

In the light of scientific investigation, the aura of supernaturalism which has engulfed the amazing faculty of psychokinesis since the earliest times has been dissolved. Controlled tests and laboratory experiments carried out in the past few decades by such notables as Dr. Rhine of Duke University have demonstrated that mind over matter is genuine, that it is a natural function of man's sixth sense which may be developed at will.

PSYCHOKINESIS: WHAT IT CAN DO FOR YOU

Unfortunately, most people do not fully understand the true value of mind over matter. The average reader may be inclined to think that it involves nothing more than using psychic energy to levitate objects or move them around in a room.

In reality, this ESP talent is far more versatile. It can be used for such diverse purposes as healing yourself and others, regulating your body temperature and even succeeding at games of chance. Psychokinesis is often used to grow healthy plants and flowers, too! The gardener on your block with the so-called green thumb is taking advantage of this hidden mental ability and may not even realize it.

Another valuable but relatively unknown aspect of mind over matter is called radiesthesia or dowsing. Through the talent, many people have been able to locate water, oil, minerals, buried treasure and other valuable resources locked away beneath the earth's surface. It is said that Caesar used radiesthesia to locate water in Rome when the aqueducts were being built, and in some areas of Africa today, dowsing is effectively used to locate oil and various minerals.

Clearly, the gift of psychokinesis is one of the most vital hidden psychic powers you possess. To develop it, you need only acquaint yourself with the easy-to-master guidelines presented in the following pages. Practice, of course, is extremely important; more so than in any other aspect of the parapsychic. But through great use and the proper mental attitude, you should be able to refine this extrasensory ability quickly and easily.

EXPERIMENT

To perform this test, you will need a pen or pencil, paper and a set of dice. Number your paper one to ten in a vertical column, then seat yourself at a table in a quiet room of your house. Take both dice into your left hand and gently close your fist.

Use perfect relaxation to remove all thoughts from your mind. When this has been done, select two numbers between one and six.

Your objective is to use the power of psychokinesis and thereby cause both dice to fall on the numbers which you have just chosen.

Using the miracle of psychic television, discussed in Chapter Two, visualize both the die in your mind as you desire them to fall. Maintain this image for approximately one minute. Also, it sometimes helps to mentally repeat the numbers forcefully several times.

Now, imagine an intense thought wave that contains the essence of your desire traveling downward from your brain, through your arm and into the dice. If you experience a peculiar sensation of warmth or a tingling in your arm, do not be alarmed; this is perfectly natural.

When ready, toss the dice before you and record the results on paper. Most likely, you will get at least one of the die correct, and perhaps both. But don't be discouraged if the results are not satisfactory. With practice, you should become more adept at this technique.

Score the results of the trial as follows: 1 point for one correct answer; 2 points if both dice fall on the specified numbers. Repeat this entire step a total of ten times so that you can obtain a realistic average, then compute your score using this table:

> 20-18 — Excellent
> 17-16 — Very good
> 15-13 — Good
> 12-9 — Average
> 8-0 — Further practice necessary.

SPECIAL INSTRUCTIONS

If your score in the preceding experiment is between 16-20, you can rest assured that you are already adept at psychokinesis and should be able to use the techniques outlined in the final half of this chapter with insured success.

If your score falls between 15-13, you should be able to use psychokinesis whenever desired; however, one half-hour of practice on the preceding step is recommended before continuing.

If your score is between 12-9, you should practice the above experiment until your accuracy shows consistent improvement. Do not attempt to use any of the following techniques until you have completed this first step.

If your score was eight or less, any one of several things could be wrong. Either you did not perform the experiment according to directions, or you were trying too hard. Just relax, carefully carry out each step of the exercise without hurrying, and your score should automatically improve.

USING PSYCHOKINETIC POWER

Rather than attempting to present a generalized formula for employing the power of psychokinesis, which cannot be done effectively, I have compiled a series of informative passages revealing the most important uses. To derive maximum benefit from this amazing ESP ability, follow all instructions and be confident of your success. Above all, practice continually so that your psychokinetic talents will have a chance to develop.

HOW TO HEAL YOURSELF

It is a scientifically proven fact that the human mind controls the bodily functions. It has also been demonstrated that psychokinesis may be used to cure, or at least relieve, certain kinds of physiological disorders, such as colds, flu, headache, nausea, stiff muscles and like afflictions.

This technique, if properly applied, will assist you in combating or completely curing the above mentioned discomforts; also, it can be used to accelerate the healing of small cuts and bruises. The method has been used by some individuals to cure serious ailments, but you should *never* try to do this yourself. Chronic conditions require a physician's attention. Therefore, use psychokinesis only in the treatment of minor ailments for which you would not ordinarily consult a doctor.

To cure aches and pains, headache or stomach upset, lie down in a quiet, darkened room and achieve perfect relaxation. This will most likely be difficult due to your physical condition; however, do the best you can.

Focus your attention on the sore area and imagine an aura of brilliant gold light enveloping that part of your body. For instance, if your shoulder hurts, surround the entire region with this powerful thought energy. For a headache, envision the gold light as a helmet-like bubble engulfing your head.

Within a minute or two, the pain should gradually begin to subside. You may feel a warm, tingling sensation in the afflicted area. Or you might experience a pleasant, cool numbness. Concentrate on this feeling and maintain the golden healing aura for a full five minutes more. At the end of this time, the discomfort should be greatly diminished or altogether gone.

You may use this same technique to speed the healing of wounds and bruises. Follow the procedure outlined above and you might be amazed to discover that minor sores disappear two or three times faster than normal, frequently overnight.

The method may also effectively alleviate hay fever, anxiety, indigestion, cramps, nausea and like disorders.

Remember: If you have the slightest suspicion that your ailment could be chronic, see a doctor at once. After you have received professional treatment, you may use psychokinesis in the above-mentioned way to speed your recovery. Much to the surprise of your attendant physician, you may be up and around in a miraculously short time!

HOW TO HEAL OTHER PEOPLE

In the same way that you can cure minor discomforts in yourself, you can also use psychokinesis to heal other people. Before you attempt to relieve someone else's pain, though, remember the precautions in the above passage. Also, to avoid possible legal repercussions, you would be wise to limit your healing assignments to close friends and relatives.

To heal minor aches and pains, cramps, cuts, contusions and like afflictions in another person, simply instruct the individual to lie down and relax completely. Shut off all the lights in the room, then situate yourself approximately three feet away from the man or woman to be healed. Determine the exact location of the pain and envelop the entire region with the golden healing aura, which as you discovered above, is nothing more than concentrated thought energy.

After a minute has gone by, ask how the individual feels: If the discomfort has not yet begun to subside, increase your concentration and intensify the gold light.

When a total of five minutes has gone by, permit the aura to slowly dissolve. Turn on a dim light and again inquire as to the person's condition. If you have performed this step correctly, he or she should report drastic improvement.

HOW TO HEAL GRAVE ILLNESS OR INJURY

Certain religious sects believe that mind over matter can be used to heal virtually any wound or disease. Conversely, those of the medical profession denounce the concept of psychic healing, claiming that drugs and medical treatment are the only genuine cures.

Personally, I have found from past experience that medical technology and psychokinesis can work together to promote swift recovery and avert complications. In fact, I have been involved in several cases where a man or a woman close to death has miraculously responded to physio-psychic treatment and gone on to live a healthy existence.

Of course, only a licensed doctor of medicine may legally prescribe treatment for the ill. The law provides harsh penalties for the unqualified practice of medicine.

However, if one of your friends or relatives becomes hospitalized due to serious illness or accident, you may still use psychokinetic power to help save the person's life or speed his recovery. This can be done legally and effectively without anyone knowing. Here is how:

From a quiet room in your home, tune in on the hospitalized person via the miracle of psychic television. When a clear image of the man or woman registers in your mind, be prepared to maintain it for five or ten minutes.

Having accomplished this, surround the individual's entire body with the healing aura of gold light. Be sure that this thought energy engulfs the person from head to toe. Do not permit the aura to weaken or dissolve at any time.

At the conclusion of five or ten minutes, blank your mind and resume your normal affairs. You may repeat this procedure three or four times each day, or more often if you desire.

Naturally, there is no such thing as a miracle, and psychokinetic power does not promise to reverse potent forces which are beyond mortal man's control. However, this healing method can certainly do no harm, and much good could result. The technique has been used by hundreds of people, including myself, and satisfactory results have been realized.

HOW TO LOCATE
WATER UNDERGROUND

By using an extra sensory ability called dowsing it is possible to locate underground springs and wells. This form of psychokinetic power is used extensively in desert regions of Africa as well as on other continents. Farmers and ranchers in parts of the midwestern United States sometimes rely on dowsing when the existing water supply is limited. In fact, the technique has proven so efficacious that some farmers actually hire professional dowsers to locate hidden springs and wells.

To perform water dowsing, you naturally must stand in a wide open place, preferably in the country. A spacious pasture, field or meadow would be ideal, or any isolated part of the desert. For equipment, you must have what is called a divining rod. This is merely a forked piece of wood, preferably pine or willow, measuring about two feet in length.

Hold the divining rod in your right hand so that the two forks are pointed toward the earth. Extend your arm and begin walking very slowly in any direction.

As you approach an underground source of water, the divining rod should begin to gently vibrate. When you are standing directly over the body of water, your rod will vibrate more intensely than before and seem to be magnetically attracted toward the earth. Of course, if there is no water nearby nothing will happen.

HOW TO LOCATE
UNDERGROUND MINERALS

A variation of dowsing may also be used to pinpoint the exact location of underground minerals and chemicals. Follow the same technique described in the above passage; however, replace the forked piece of wood with a copper rod measuring about two feet in length and one-half inch in diameter. It is not necessary that this special divining rod be forked, but it does help.

THE AMAZING DOWSING PENDULUM

Another amazing device used to locate mineral deposits is called the dowsing pendulum. Some people claim it is even more efficacious than the above mentioned technique.

You can make a dowsing pendulum from materials most likely to be found in your own home. All you need is a chain from a necklace and a small pendant made of the mineral you seek to locate. For example, if you desire to use dowsing to locate an underground deposit of iron, attach a small object made of that ore to an end of the chain.

Take the dowsing pendulum to an isolated area, such as in the mountains, and stand in an open place. Let the chain dangle loosely in your right hand and wait for it to stop swaying.

Now, concentrate on the particular mineral you seek. Close your eyes for about a minute and visualize the exact pendant which is mounted to the chain. Slowly at first, the pendulum will begin to swing back and forth. When you open your eyes, you should be able to perceive it being magnetically attracted to a particular direction.

Without interrupting the motion of the pendulum, slowly proceed in the designated way. When you are in close proximity to a deposit of the desired mineral, the pendant will suddenly move around in eratic circles. If no such ore is buried in your vicinity, the pendulum will not work.

This technique requires practice, but once you become adept at it, you should be able to use the dowsing pendulum and realize amazing results with great ease.

THE SECRET OF THE GREEN THUMB

Have you ever wondered why some people seem to be gifted with a green thumb at gardening, while others have trouble just growing a lawn or shrubbery?

Fertilizer, soil conditions and proper watering are to some extent responsible, but the real secret is: psychokinesis.

Plants are acutely sensitive to human thought impulses. This claim is not the product of an overactive imagination, but has been conclusively demonstrated time and again in laboratories throughout the world. Researchers have attached sophisticated electronic equipment such as the polygraph to the leaves and stems of various species of flora, and found that all plants actually register feelings.

What's more incredible, science now knows that virtually every flowering plant and vegetable can interpret a human's unspoken emotions and respond accordingly. In other words, a plant can tell how you feel about it! If you dislike it, it will not flourish as well as plants you like.

This explains why some people have better luck at gardening than others: By using mind over matter and transmitting positive thoughts, garden vegetation can be made to thrive. The man or woman who lacks the proper attitude can never expect to cultivate a healthy garden, no matter how much fertilizer and water is invested.

While this may seem like a concept straight from a science fiction writer's notebook, I assure you it is quite the opposite. In fact, there is an easy way you can prove this amazing discovery to your own satisfaction. Just carry out the following experiment and you will see how the power of psychokinesis influences a plant's growth.

EXPERIMENT

Purchase two identical flowerpots and a packet of daisies from your local grocery store or nursery. Fill each planter with the same amount of dirt and plant three or four seeds in each. Place both flowerpots together and give each an identical amount of water. This may be best accomplished by using a measuring cup.

Having performed this step according to directions, it would be logical to assume that both planters should produce identical results. All of the flowers should germinate in the same period of time, sprout and grow in an identical manner.

Label one flowerpot "A", and the other "B". Be sure that you do not confuse them in the days ahead.

The day after, kneel before planter A and send positive thoughts to those seeds. Envision them sprouting and rapidly developing into healthy specimens in record time. Continue transmitting these thoughts for exactly five minutes. Then turn to planter B and do the opposite. Send negative thoughts to those seeds. Imagine yourself stabbing at the ground; envision the plants growing and see yourself ripping their leaves away and breaking the stems. Think of these particular plants as ugly, to be destroyed upon sight. Consider them enemies and mentally command them not to grow. At the end of exactly five minutes, resume your normal activities.

Repeat this entire step each and every day for about two weeks, or longer if necessary. First, send positive thoughts to the seeds in planter A, then negative thoughts to those in the second flowerpot.

Soon you will begin to see the results of this experiment. The daisies in planter A will sprout long before the others, will grow taller and healthier, and generally flourish. Those in planter B will be late to sprout, if they do so at all. They will be scrawny and unproductive. Although they may sprout, they may wither and die soon thereafter.

You can draw your own conclusions from this amazing experiment. If you wish, repeat the entire procedure again to verify the results; but each time, the same thing will occur. The plants receiving your positive thoughts will flourish, while the others will barely sustain themselves.

Why? Logically, the phenomena cannot be explained. Both planters were exposed to identical physical conditions—identical amounts of water, sunlight, etc. Both were planted at the same time, in the same amount and type of soil, and the seeds were taken from the same packet. Yet, a drastic difference in the growth rate and productivity between the two planters occurred.

There is only one feasible explanation: the power of mind over matter.

Chapter Six

How To Send ESP Messages Through Space

Man's inborn capacity to consciously project telepathic messages through space and have them received by other people constitutes nothing more than mind reading in reverse. Yet this extrasensory power, called active telepathy, has been identified with various magic and spiritualist cult practices, and therefore condemned, for countless centuries. Political and religious leaders of all persuasions, especially those in power throughout the medieval era in Europe, considered this particular psychic talent to be more evil than most. Fanatics adamantly insisted that it was an intangible gift bestowed by the devil and hence unsafe for the loyal, rank and file citizens.

The alleged consequences incurred through the use of this rudimentary psychic power are repeatedly defined in many old records. Sorcerers and cultist priests in league with Satan were said to have used active telepathy to control the minds of leading officials. Further, such rebels reputedly employed the power to implant decadent thoughts in the minds of the pure, confuse those functionaries who sought to expose them, and transmit feelings of malcontent into the collective mind of the populace.

These and a host of similar allegations, circulated by supporters of the ruling class who at the same time envied and feared so-called supernatural phenomena, propelled the uneducated masses to the brink of hysteria and subsequently triggered the bloodiest purge known to history: the Inquisition.

ACTIVE TELEPATHY DEFINED

Fortunately, twentieth century technology has prevailed over superstition and we Americans are free to pursue psychic development. ESP researchers, who would have been deemed heretics and burned a few centuries ago, are now able to sift through the existing data and have done much in recent years to help us distinguish fact from fiction.

Mankind presently has access to the most extensive store of knowledge on parapsychological phenomena ever to exist. And among those extrasensory characteristics now documented and commonly accepted as genuine, is one innocuous and potentially valuable power: active telepathy.

This particular mental ability, like all others discussed in this text, has nothing to do with the supernatural. It is a perfectly normal function of the sixth sense which may be consciously unlocked and cultivated. There are no inherent dangers, and you should encounter no adverse side effects.

You may be surprised to know that the powers of active telepathy and mind reading are in essence the same. Both function in accordance with like principles and conjointly render two-way mental communication possible. The sole difference rests in the fact that one involves receiving thoughts, while the other is primarily concerned with sending them. Hence, if you have familiarized yourself with the fundamentals of mind reading and taken the time to practice, the new talent should blossom rapidly. Once you have mastered several elementary techniques which, except for a few slight modifications, are identical to the ones you have already learned, the power of active telepathy will be at your fingertips.

WHAT ACTIVE TELEPATHY CAN DO FOR YOU

This type of ESP is surprisingly versatile and a host of practical applications therefore exist. Of course, no one can tell you how or when to employ your power, so the benefits which you derive in the final analysis will depend largely on your individual needs and ambitions. Provided you observe the limits of common sense and discretion at all times, active telepathy can be nothing but constructive and will serve to your advantage.

Suffice it to say, space does not permit a thorough listing of every possible application, but a few examples are presented here in order to give you a better idea of how valuable this hidden psychic power may prove to be.

DISASTER NARROWLY AVERTED

One striking incident that illustrates the efficacy of active telepathy occurred in mid-August of 1971. Vincent R., an acquaintance of mine, had his car in a local garage for repairs and borrowed a relative's second car in the interim. It was in poor running condition, but it enabled him to commute to and from work until his own automobile was operating.

One afternoon, without warning, a series of vivid impressions flooded my mind. I mentally perceived my friend involved in a disastrous auto accident less than a block from his office. I remember thinking at the time that his brakes had gone out.

In the past, I had experienced similar phenomena, and in each instance the impressions proved to be precognitive warnings. I stopped at a public phone booth and tried to call Vincent on the job, but a particularly obstinate secretary informed me that he was at a meeting and could not be disturbed for *any* reason. When I returned home thirty minutes later, I tried to call again but still could not get through.

As a last resort, I used the power of active telepathy and conveyed an intense warning thought, repeating in my mind: "Vincent ... check your brakes ... the brakes on your car may go out ..."

Later that evening, my friend telephoned, sounding quite astonished. He reported that he had heard my voice earlier in the day, telling him to check the brakes on his car. He had indeed been tied up at a staff meeting when my thoughts registered, but immediately afterward, he rushed to the parking lot and discovered that his brake fluid had leaked out.

Had he attempted to drive the automobile, a collision would have been inevitable.

MARRIAGE PROPOSED BY ACTIVE TELEPATHY!

Robert N., a close friend whom I had known since my freshman year in high school, revealed to me that he used active telepathy to propose marriage!

Robert, who was a likable but basically shy individual, explained that he had tried to propose to Sandy W. on several occasions but could not find the right words. Finally, one night after a date, he used a technique I had taught him previously and sent this telepathic message to the girl: "Sandy.... This is Robert speaking.... I want to marry you...." He repeated this exact phrase in his mind for about ten minutes, then fell asleep.

The following afternoon when they met, Sandy reported that she had experienced an unusual hallucination in which she heard Robert talking to her the night before! This broke the ice and after considerable hedging, my friend succeeded in formalizing the engagement and was married three months later.

THE HIDDEN POWER YOU NOW POSSESS

As you already know, thought constitutes a pure form of energy. It is an invisible but potent force, extremely common but at the same time difficult to measure and analyze. Similarly to light rays and currents of electricity, it may be produced and channeled along a specific direction. So, just as it is possible to focus a beam of light on a precise target area, your thought can be aimed at any person of your choice and received clearly. This is exactly what happens in active telepathy.

Your thought waves apparently travel at a velocity equal to the speed of light: an incredible 186,000 miles per second. This belief is based on the fact that most genuine reports of psychic phenomena seem to indicate that thought transference occurs almost instantaneously. Hence, a well-directed telepathic message can travel all the way around the world in a fraction of a second, if you know how to project it.

Any unspoken idea, feeling or desire that passes through your mind is called a thought, and it can be mentally conveyed to other people without your speaking. However, our thoughts are ordinarily too fragmented and weak to be projected through space. We know what we think and feel in the course of daily living, but to form a telepathic message and send it haphazardly is by no means the key to active telepathy.

Any unspoken message must have three qualities in order to be received and interpreted by another person. First, it must be well-aimed so the desired person and no one else will perceive it. Second, it must contain a single thought wholly apart from any other feelings or ideas you may be currently experiencing. And, lastly, it must be strong enough to register clearly in the other person's mind with definite impact. Lacking this final quality, any message you send could be easily ignored or overlooked.

When you have a particular thought, place it foremost in your mind and eliminate all others, then amplify it so that it becomes highly intense. You have created what is called a thought form. This is the secret of active telepathy, for such an impulse may be quickly and easily created, then projected to the desired individual without losing its intensity in the process.

Generally, thought forms are of two types: emotional and controlled. Once you have learned how to produce these and send them through space, you will be a master at active telepathy.

To familiarize yourself with this unique concept, here is an experiment with emotional thought forms, which are the most elementary.

EXPERIMENT

Have you ever encountered a stranger who seemed to be projecting an intense wave of hostility or warmth aimed directly at you? Chances are this has happened to you more than once. If so, you have received an emotional thought form without even realizing it. Such a mental impulse does not contain a specific message but merely conveys one person's feelings to another. The phenomena is especially pronounced between intimate friends and lovers, who are so acutely attuned to each other that telepathic transference of emotion occurs without conscious effort.

You can see how this operates by performing the following experiment.

For this test, you will need the cooperation of a very close friend or relative. Your spouse, fiance or lover would be ideal. Retire to a quiet room of your home and sit facing each other about five feet apart. Get comfortable and relax.

Instruct your partner to try and blank all conscious thought from his or her mind. Then have the person concentrate intently on some past experience which evoked deep emotion: for example, a death in the family, a love affair, a very pleasant memory, etc. Tell your partner to relive the event mentally and to think of nothing but.

When this has been done, the two of you should meet and lock eyes. Do not stare unblinkingly as this will only distract you. Simply relax and gaze, deeply and intently.

Eliminate all thought from your own mind using perfect relaxation. Having performed this step, leave your mind open to anything that may enter it.

Within a few seconds, you should suddenly experience a deep and intense emotion being projected by your partner. For instance, if the person chooses a pleasant memory upon which to dwell, you will know it and sense joy coming into your mind. Conversely, if your partner chose a tragic incident, you will perceive sadness.

Such an intense telepathic message is called a thought form, being of an emotional nature in this case.

When you have terminated the experiment, you and your partner should compare notes to verify the validity of the impressions you received. If you desire, repeat the experiment several times more. This is a good practice exercise and it will enable you to become more familiar with the concept of sending and receiving thought forms.

HOW TO CREATE AND PROJECT EMOTIONAL THOUGHT FORMS

If you are like most people, you have probably known many occasions when you wanted to convey a particular feeling to a friend or stranger, yet for some reason could not do so. Either you could not find the proper words to make your thoughts known, or communication simply did not exist.

Now, through the revolutionary concept of emotional thought forms, you can impress intense feelings in the minds of people you choose. To create and project such impulses, simply observe this easy, step-by-step procedure. Practice it, and in a matter of days you will be able to telepathically broadcast your feelings in no more than a few seconds.

First: Decide upon the type of emotional thought form you wish to transmit, whether affection, hostility, trust, or some other feeling.

Second: Use perfect relaxation to completely subdue your mind and body.

Third: Hold the emotional feeling you wish to convey uppermost in your mind and concentrate on nothing else. Until you become adept at this technique, it may be advisable for you to recall some past experience which evoked the particular emotion desired. Focus your complete attention on this feeling for about a minute and you will have created a thought form.

Fourth: To project this impulse to a person who is nearby, say, in the same room, all you need to do is touch the person briefly (contact telepathy), or meet and lock eyes for approximately ten seconds. This will establish a psychic link between the two of you and your emotional thought form will automatically be conveyed.

(If you want to send such a thought form over a distance, or if the person in question does not happen to be in close proximity at the time, refer to a later heading in this chapter, "How To Project Controlled Thought Forms.")

EXERCISE

In order to become proficient in this amazing technique, you must naturally practice at every opportunity. Use the following exercise to refine this particular ESP talent:

When you are about to be introduced to someone, fix a specific emotional thought form uppermost in your mind as prescribed above. When you shake hands, try to catch the man or woman's eyes for a few seconds. This will facilitate physical as well as visual contact and so insure that a psychic link is established. The thought form will then be transferred from you to the other person. When this happens, the intense feeling transfixed in your mind may rapidly taper. Or the thought may dissolve instantly. In either case, you will know you have been successful.

Perform this exercise whenever you meet new people, or re-establish contact with old acquaintances. As you become more proficient in the use of the technique, you'll be able to project pleasant thought forms in a matter of seconds, making everyone you meet respond favorably and reciprocate your friendliness. The same method may be used to win someone's fondest affections, but to succeed in this you must practice constantly.

THE SECRET OF CONTROLLED THOUGHT FORMS

Beyond imparting deep and intense emotion in the manner discussed above, it is possible to transmit actual messages and suggestions through space and have them received by the people of your choice. To do so, you create and project controlled thought forms. These are generally of two types: photopic and auricular. Each variation involves the power of active telepathy. But in the first instance, an unspoken image of a suggestive nature is subtly implanted in someone's mind; in the latter case, a word or series of words comprising a message is sent. An easy way of distinguishing one from the other is to remember that photopic sounds like photo, and refers to pictorial impressions.

The auricular thought form is the most convenient, effective and direct means of telepathic communication. Examples of this method may be found in the two case studies involving my own experiences presented earlier in this chapter. Auricular, literally means "to be said privately" and is used in a psychic sense to describe an intense telepathic message consisting of words and containing the essence of a single thought. Thus, if you transmit a warning such as "Vincent . . . check the brakes on your car . . . the brakes may go out . . .," you are implementing such a thought form. The person who receives it will usually hear your voice in their mind and perceive your exact words. No one else, however, will be able to tune in on the message.

The photopic thought form, on the other hand, comprises a more indirect and subtle approach to active telepathy. It entails your visualizing someone acting in a manner which you desire, and implanting such an image in that particular person's mind. When this thought form is received, it automatically triggers a strong urge in the individual to comply with your request. This technique produces results which strongly coincide with those attained by hypnotic suggestion. Normally, the man or woman so affected will not even know that a photopic thought form has been implanted and will consider the subsequent desire to be no more than the product of his or her own mental processes.

Naturally, in using the latter technique, common sense and discretion must be applied at all times. Used constructively, tremendous value may be derived from photopic thought forms. You will be able to implant subtle suggestions in the minds of your friends and loved ones, and help them to recognize habits, shortcomings, virtues and capabilities when more conventional means of communication might prove cumbersome. You can even plant a certain thought form to assist a friend stop smoking or biting his nails. Likewise, you can use this hidden psychic power to improve your own life, gain new friends, and achieve love and ultimate fulfillment in all your undertakings.

But, like everything in life, the technique may be easily abused and set against people for destructive ends. Of course, you are certainly intelligent enough to know better. To be on the safe side, always keep the Golden Rule uppermost in your thoughts: Do unto others as you would have them do unto you. If you consistently heed this code, you will never be in jeopardy of misusing your ESP abilities: All your deeds will be constructive and rewarding.

HOW TO CREATE AN AURICULAR THOUGHT FORM

Whenever you want to project any kind of direct message through space and have it received by another person, you must first create the appropriate thought form. Use these guidelines to devise one that will satisfy your needs:

First: Write down the message that you want to send. This will help clarify the idea in your mind. Be as brief and concise as possible. Eliminate all unnecessary words as you would in preparing a telegram.

Second: Begin the thought form with the first name of the person you are sending it to, then insert the bulk of the message.

Third: Never use such words as "I" or "me". Replace all pronouns of this sort with your own name. For example, in the thought form, "Mary, write me a letter," the man or woman you are communicating with will perceive those exact words. If your voice does not register distinctly in the person's mind, the recipient—in this case, Mary—will be unable to identify "me" and therefore cannot comply with the request. This same thought form should be revised and shortened to: "Mary, write John." Or, if you wish to stress your own name, it could read: "Mary, this is John speaking. Write me". Both versions are clear and to the point. They will be easier for you to send and will be received with greater impact than a long, flowery dissertation.

Fourth: You have just created an auricular thought form. It may now be quickly conveyed, with virtually no effort, to the person of your choosing, no matter where in the world he or she may be and regardless of whether you know the individual. To find out how, consult the subheading; "How To Project Controlled Thought Forms" appearing later in this chapter.

HOW TO CREATE PHOTOPIC THOUGHT FORMS

Projecting a telepathic suggestion or command through space and implanting it in a man or woman's mind can also be accomplished with relative ease. All you must do is devise a suitable photopic thought form, then transmit it to the individual.

Remember, in this type of active telepathy you are not concerned with worded messages, but with pictorial images. You must visualize a person actually conforming to the suggestion you wish to implant and then project the essence of that thought. Hence, in the above example, "Mary, write John," you would want to envision the person sitting down at a table with paper and pen and actually inscribing the words, "Dear John," just as if doing so in real life. When such a thought form is received, the individual will suddenly feel compelled to act in accordance with the request.

To devise photopic thought forms that will fulfill your own needs, all you must do is determine the content of the suggestion to be implanted, then translate the idea into an image of the man or woman complying. It's that easy, and once you have completed this step you will be ready to actually project the message.

Presented here are a few common examples of photopic thought forms.

PHOTOPIC THOUGHT FORM NO. 1

To make a friend call you on the phone, envision the person picking up the receiver and dialing your number. When this exact image has been implanted telepathically, he or she will be possessed by a sudden desire to contact you at the first opportunity.

PHOTOPIC THOUGHT FORM NO. 2

To help someone stop smoking, envision the man or woman lighting a cigarette, coughing on its smoke, then dropping it to the ground and crushing it underfoot. Repeat this step for approximately ten minutes on several separate days and it should compel the most dedicated chain-smoker to quit!

HOW TO PROJECT CONTROLLED THOUGHT FORMS

Now that you are sufficiently knowledgeable in the concept of thought forms, you are ready to begin using active telepathy to broadcast your thoughts to others. If you have taken the time to study the information presented earlier in this chapter, you should encounter no difficulty in applying what you know.

You may be surprised to discover that thought forms can be projected through space, regardless of the distance involved, as easily as they are created. Simply observe the following guidelines and you will be able to make full use of this amazing psychic power.

STEP NO. 1

Decide upon the content of the thought form to be sent. Work out all the details beforehand using the information presented in the preceding sections. Then, commit the exact message to memory so that you will not overlook crucial points in the process of transmitting it.

STEP NO. 2

Retire to a quiet place where you will be

able to concentrate without distraction. A darkened room, cool and well-ventilated, would prove ideal. Make yourself comfortable in an armchair or on a sofa. Relax every muscle in your body and clear all thoughts and anxiety from your mind. Use perfect relaxation to achieve the desired state.

Remember, the degree of success you encounter in the use of active telepathy depends largely on the intensity of your thought forms. Those which are weak most likely will not register in a person's conscious mind. The key to satisfactory results is absolute concentration. And therefore you must be completely tranquil and at ease.

STEP NO. 3

Use standard visualization to transfix a vivid image of the person you want to communicate with in your mind's eye. Concentrate intently on the individual's face, gazing into his or her eyes for approximately two or three minutes. At the end of this time, you will have established an invisible psychic link between the two of you.

STEP NO. 4

Follow the instructions pertaining to the type of thought form you intend to utilize.

Emotional: Direct an intense wave of the desired emotion to the person's image. If you want to send love, for example, continue visualizing as directed and at the same time permit a strong feeling of warmth and affection to permeate your thoughts. The exact emotion you project in this manner will be perceived by the individual within a few seconds, regardless of his or her location or present activities.

Auricular: Continue visualizing in the prescribed manner. At the same time, focus your thoughts on the message to be projected and repeat each word clearly and forcefully in your mind. Hence, if you want a friend to call you, keep his or her face in your thoughts and strongly think: "Mary, call John." While still visualizing, repeat the phrase again and again for about five or ten minutes. When you suddenly experience a sensation of relief, or light-headedness, you will know that the thought form has been perceived. This usually occurs within the above mentioned time period, give or take a few minutes depending on the intensity of your thought.

Photopic: To implant this type of thought form, all that is required is a simple technique. Mentally, see the person's image conforming to your request. For example, to make a person call you, visualize him moving toward a telephone, picking up the receiver and dialing your number. Repeatedly visualize this scene in detail from beginning to end for about ten minutes. This should allow sufficient time to implant the desired suggestion. In the case of an unusually complicated photopic thought form, or one that a person would be inclined to reject —such as a smoker giving up cigarettes—repeat the entire step for several consecutive days for best results.

Properly applied, the guidelines and techniques presented in this chapter should enable you to send your thoughts to other people across the world. You will be able to communicate with friends and relatives, contemporaries and strangers. You may wish to make active telepathy a part of your day-to-day existence, or you might decide to use this unique psychic power only in times of emergency. That is entirely up to you.

But, remember, only through practice will you become truly adept. Proficiency is the result of experience and it is not usually acquired overnight.

Chapter Seven

How To Receive Messages
From the Spirit World

Does the spirit world really exist? Can man transcend the so-called fourth dimension and communicate with discarnate entities—the spirits of deceased friends and loved ones?

According to science, the answer is an emphatic no. Leading members of the intellectual community officially denounce the concept of the spirit world and say that people who claim to be in contact with the dead are either charlatans or are hallucinating.

Yet there are some documented accounts of ethereal phenomena which defy logical explanation. Scores of men and women from every walk of life have received amazing messages from "beyond" through devices such as the popular Ouija board. And many thousands more who have participated in seances acknowledge that they have verified the validity of spirit communication to their own satisfaction. Even devout skeptics have been visibly shaken by the incredible phenomenon witnessed during such meetings.

The purpose of this chapter, however, is not to argue for or against the existence of discarnate entities, but to reveal a set of guidelines, which, if properly applied, may enable you to transcend the fourth dimension. You are not asked to believe in the intriguing concept of spirit communication, but you are urged to maintain an open mind and reserve final judgment until you have experimented with the techniques presented here.

It is impossible to know beforehand what kind of results you will achieve. Perhaps, like some people, you will come away believing that the spirit realm is purely imaginary. Or you may encounter astonishing evidence and so prove to your own satisfaction that the fourth dimension is indeed a reality.

Try these unique exercises and see.

HOW TO CONVERSE
WITH THE SPIRIT WORLD

The two most common methods employed in communicating with discarnate entities are the Ouija board and the traditional seance. Both of these have been repeatedly examined in other texts on ESP and so repetition here is unwarranted. Suffice it to say that there are countless ways of conducting a seance, usually under the supervision of a trained medium; and the operation of the Ouija board is based on a technique which anyone could master in about ten seconds.

At present we are primarily concerned with several other obscure but fascinating methods of contacting the invisible world which have been virtually ignored by most contemporary authorities. The first is automatic writing, which involves your recording actual messages channeled through your subconscious mind by discarnate entities. The second means relies on an easy-to-make device, the psychic pendulum. Through this astonishing pendulum, you can obtain answers to thousands of easily-posed questions.

Both of these phenomena are discussed at length in the following passages, and helpful guidelines for taking advantage of them are also included. However, it must again be emphasized that an open mind and a sense of honest expectation are prerequisites if you hope to realize meaningful results. As stated before, absolute belief is not mandatory, but if your skepticism is extremely strong, it can interfere with a positive outcome.

AUTOMATIC WRITING: WHAT IT IS

Imagine being able to sit down at your desk with pen and paper in hand, doodle aimlessly for a few minutes and discover that you have unconsciously penned an intelligible message from the spirit world!

Impossible?

The enigma of automatic writing has baffled researchers for years. Many experts denounce the phenomenon as a hoax, while others surmise that messages produced in this manner are the product of subconscious activity, possibly coupled with memory or extrasensory perception.

The latter theory could be true in the case of Evelyn W., an Illinois housewife whose eldest teenage son ran away from home in the spring of 1972. After several weeks, police in the area were unable to ascertain the boy's whereabouts, and several psychics enlisted by the distraught mother also failed to provide a clue. One afternoon, the woman was doodling to relieve her anxiety. When she glanced down at the sheet of paper, she discovered that a hotel address and room number in New York City had been scrawled in her mother's hand. Oddly enough, her mother had died several years before. Acting on a hunch, she contacted the police in New York, who investigated her report and located the missing teenager at that precise address.

Granted, this woman could have subconsciously reproduced her deceased relative's handwriting based on past memory. And ESP could have enabled her to ascertain the address of her missing son.

But what about the case of one Thomas James, a man whose education had ended in his early teens yet who, in the year 1873, completed a novel, *The Mystery of Edwin Drood*, with the same depth and precision demonstrated by the famous author who had started the manuscript but died before it could be finished—Charles Dickens.

A year after Dickens' death, James coincidentally began attending seances at his hometown in Vermont. One evening he suddenly announced that he was communicating with the spirit of Charles Dickens and had been asked to finish writing *The Mystery of Edwin Drood* under the discarnate entity's guidance. Witnesses later reported that James spent hours in a semi-trance state, day after day receiving entire manuscript pages through automatic writing. A year later, when the completed novel appeared on the newsstands, skeptics were astonished. One critic raved that "only Dickens himself could have written it."

Yet Dickens was dead. And James, a practically illiterate printer who never wrote another book or article in his life, had indeed penned the conclusion to the novel.

AN EXPERIMENT
WITH AUTOMATIC WRITING

Here is an easy experiment you can perform with automatic writing. Of course, there is no sure way to know what kind of results you will encounter. Unlike other aspects of parapsychology discussed earlier, this particular phenomenon does not seem to conform with the laws of physical science, nor is it fully understood. Yet, automatic writing does work for some people—and it could work for you.

To perform this experiment, simply adhere to the following instructions:

1) Retire, with paper and pencil, to a quiet room in your home. Be certain that the location you select will be completely free from distractions, preferably cool and well-ventilated. Close the curtains and switch off all lights so that the place will be dark, then situate yourself at a desk or table.

2) Get comfortable. Use perfect relaxation to subdue your mind and body. Expel all tension and anxiety as these will tend to interfere with the experiment. Just relax completely and think of nothing.

3) When the desired state has been achieved,

reach out and take the pencil into your hand. Touch the tip of it to your paper, then relax your arm. You should be able to perceive no sensation whatsoever in either that hand or arm. The entire side of your body should be pleasantly numb.

4) Imagine that you are gently drifting in a blackened void. Command yourself to hear and feel absolutely nothing. After several minutes, vague images may begin to form in your mind. Do not expel them. Just stay relaxed and observe. Continue this step for approximately thirty minutes without interruption. If you have performed this exercise correctly and your hand begins to move and produce a message, you should be unaware of it.

5) In the half-hour interim of Step Four, any forthcoming missives from the spirit world should have been received. Therefore, switch on a light and examine the paper on your desk. Are there any markings on the sheet? If not, try to avoid becoming discouraged. This, like all other things, requires practice.

If you achieved no results at all, or if the page is filled with aimless doodles and designs, it could be that your conscious mind is interfering with reception of ethereal transmissions. Therefore, perform the above experiment again, passing slowly and carefully from one step to the next.

THE AMAZING PSYCHIC PENDULUM

The psychic pendulum is a simple device consisting of a chain from a necklace and a small pendant featuring your birthstone. It may be used to contact the spirit realm and obtain "yes" or "no" answers to any questions you could conceivably pose.

The pendulum, like automatic writing, has worked for thousands of people, but science does not know why. Theories have been advanced, but there is no substantiating evidence. Some say that discarnate entities influence the pendulum's operation, while others attribute the phenomena to subconscious energy. The truth is yet to emerge.

My own initial experience with the psychic pendulum occurred early in 1968. A friend had introduced me to the device weeks before, but I did not consider it seriously. Then, one evening, several friends and I were passing through a desert town north of Los Angeles. The car radiator overheated and we stopped at a cafe for coffee. As a practical joke, I pulled my pendulum, given to me as a gift weeks earlier, from my coat pocket. Using the device as instructed, I asked: "Will we get back to Los Angeles tonight?" The answer was "no." "Will we have more car trouble?" was my second question, and the pendulum answered, "yes".

One of my friends, being a devout skeptic, grinned and queried: "Ask if we'll get out of the cafe parking lot." I did, and the answer was "no". Twenty minutes later, we left the restaurant and got into our car. It refused to start. The driver lifted up the hood and made a cursory inspection. In the process, he shattered the fuel pump bowl. We were indeed stranded in the parking lot and did not return to Los Angeles until the next morning. Of course, it could have been coincidence, but since that time many similar events have transpired, reinforcing my faith in the efficacy of the pendulum.

You, too, can make your own psychic pendulum and take advantage of this simple but effective device. All you need to do is determine your personal birthstone from the chart below, attach the appropriate gem to a thin chain and use it in accordance with the following directions.

TABLE OF THE BIRTHSTONES

ARIES	- Diamond	LIBRA	- Opal
TAURUS	- Emerald	SCORPIO	- Topaz
GEMINI	- Agate	SAGITTARIUS	- Turquoise
CANCER	- Ruby	CAPRICORN	- Garnet
LEO	- Sardonyx	AQUARIUS	- Amethyst
VIRGO	- Sapphire	PISCES	- Bloodstone

A psychic pendulum consisting of a pendant that features your personal birthstone previously worn by a friend or relative now deceased is especially powerful.

HOW TO USE YOUR PSYCHIC PENDULUM

Once you have obtained the necessary materials and assembled your own pendulum, you should wear it around your neck constantly except when it is in use. Also, avoid letting other people come in contact with the pendant as this may tend to interfere with its operation.

To use your psychic pendulum, follow these steps:

First: Hold the chain lightly between the thumb and forefinger of your right hand, allowing the birthstone to dangle freely at one end. Anchor your arm on a table or some other hard surface and wait for the pendulum to stop swinging and come to a perfect standstill.

Second: Verbally ask any question that can be answered, "yes" or "no". State your question clearly and simply. Then watch what happens.

Third: Even though your hand is perfectly motionless, the pendulum will begin to swing, gradually at first but with increasing force. Its movement provides the answer to your question. If it swings to and from your body, it indicates a "yes" response; if from left to right, a "no" is the answer. If the pendant zigzags around in erratic patterns, it means that you have asked a foolish question to which you already know the answer. This is an example of humor from the spirit world!

By following the same step-by-step procedure you may ask as many questions as desired on practically any subject—even what the future holds in store. With practice, you can become highly proficient at using the psychic pendulum and achieving amazingly accurate results.

You now have at your disposal two unique secrets that will, if properly applied and practiced, permit you to transcend the fourth dimension.

Whether you do or do not choose to believe in the existence of a spirit world populated by invisible entities is a matter of individual choice. Granted, the concept is a difficult one to accept and you may seek some other explanation for the phenomena of automatic writing and the psychic pendulum.

Yet, when you have become thoroughly familiar with the fine points of these techniques and become accustomed to using them as an integral part of your daily life, you may well come to the realization, like many other people, that such a dimension does indeed exist.

Time, and your own personal experience, will resolve the question.

Chapter Eight

Have You Lived Before?

It may seem ironic in this technologically advanced world of miracle drugs and space flight that the concept of reincarnation has become deeply entrenched in the mainstream of our civilization. With the vast array of modern conveniences readily available today for the asking, one might be inclined to think that most men and women would have no urgent desire to remember past life experiences, if there is in fact such a past to contemplate. It would seem as though we should be content in present time.

Yet, many of us are not. The theory of rebirth fascinates a wide assortment of people in this society. No matter where you may go today, you are bound to encounter a score of average men and women who adamantly insist that they have lived on this earth before. Virtually thousands have experienced memories of their distant past, and many more people are attempting to find out how they may begin to remember even the most vague incidents of a previous existence.

The incredible advance of technology in comparatively recent times is largely responsible for the widespread interest in reincarnation. Although science has placed man on the moon, discovered the secret of the atom and may soon be able to manufacture life in a test tube, it has at the same time pushed man to the brink of a new spiritual horizon. People no different from you and I are beginning to ask: "Why was I born? What is my purpose, or do I even have one?" Are we to assume that we are born of sexual union between a male and a female, and that in an uncertain length of time each of us will die and merely rot away in our graves? Or is there some greater purpose to life, some far-reaching significance which cannot be examined under a microscope?

The theory of reincarnation states that every man, woman and child now alive has undergone a series of previous lifetimes. We are, according to the belief, continually born into this world to advance and mature spiritually. Those who are acquainted with the theory see life as a long upward climb from total imperfection—in the first life—to ultimate perfection and illumination, at which point the need for an individual to be reborn terminates.

Reincarnation, if it is a reality, could provide the answers to many of man's unanswered questions. Let us assume for a moment that we actually survive through a continuous string of physical embodiments to satisfy the cycle of rebirth. This could explain why some people are more psychically gifted and intellectually advanced than others, more gifted and capable. It would explain why every so often an Einstein or a Da Vinci appears on this planet. It would also explain why we are what we are and give reason to the circumstances, both good and bad, each of us may encounter in the course of our existence.

You are not asked to believe in the concept of reincarnation solely on the basis of blind faith. In fact, you are not asked to believe in this intriguing theory at all. But you are urged to approach the question with an open mind, and to reserve judgment until you have experimented with the guidelines presented below. If you have in fact lived before, these guidelines will permit you to find out.

Reincarnation cannot be scientifically proven and evaluated. The evidence that exists seems to strongly indicate that rebirth is distinctly possible, but in the final analysis belief is a matter of your own choice.

Therefore, try applying these step-by-step-guidelines and see what happens. You may decide that the theory of rebirth is imaginary. Or you might prove to yourself that it is genuine.

HOW TO REMEMBER

There are various ways to investigate the phenomenon of reincarnation, some more elaborate and time-consuming than others. Regression by means of hypnosis is probably the most popular technique, but it is also extremely dangerous, even when attempted by professionals in a controlled environment. Serious psychological after effects have been reported by more than one half of the people who have been subjected to hypnotically induced memory.

The safest way to recall past life experiences, and perhaps the easiest, is by relying on natural capabilities of the human mind. In other words, it is possible to delve into your distant past without using artificial stimuli such as drugs and hypnosis. Through spontaneous recall, conjointly used with deep meditation, you should be able to safely and easily recall past lives, if you have lived them, with complete clarity.

How can you remember?

Simply observe these step-by-step guidelines.

STEP NO. 1

Retire to a quiet, well-ventilated room in your home where you will be able to spend an hour's time uninterrupted. Close all the curtains, switch off the lights, then lie down flat on your back, either on a bed, a sofa or the floor. Use perfect relaxation to tranquilize your mind and body. Be absolutely certain that every muscle is limp and your thoughts subdued before proceeding to the next step. Avoid being tense or anxious as these conditions will only interfere with your success.

STEP NO. 2

Inhale slowly and gently to the count of ten. Hold your breath for three counts, then exhale again to the count of ten. This exercise, called deep breathing, is a further aid to total relaxation and will permit you to temporarily blank your conscious mind to the fullest extent.

Repeat this exercise for approximately two minutes, then go on to the next step.

STEP NO. 3

Using the technique of standard visualization, which was revealed earlier in this text, transfix the face of a clock in your mind's eye. Envision the second hand slowly moving *backwards*, and the minute hand corresponding, going back one minute for each sixty seconds. This will permit you to actually program your subconscious mind to journey back through time. Continue this step for approximately ten minutes, then go on to Step No. 4.

STEP NO. 4

Clear your mind again, and imagine that you are silently drifting in a cool, blackened void. You should hear no sounds and perceive no physical sensation beyond that of lightness. Simply drift in this manner for five or ten minutes.

STEP NO. 5

Now, visualize some pleasant event that took place in your life within the past month. As clearly and precisely as possible, actually envision yourself reliving that particular experience.

Adhering to these same instructions, relive a pleasant event that occurred about one year ago, then five years, ten years and, finally some pleasant childhood experience. For best results, proceed slowly and carefully, spending as much time as required to perform each phase of this exercise.

STEP NO. 6

Once again, blank your mind and imagine that you are floating in a blackened void. Just drift aimlessly along and allow a sense of tranquility to overpower you. Within a few minutes, vague images may begin to register in your mind. You may see faces, locations and hear voices that you have never seen or heard before. Do absolutely nothing but observe, as these peculiar images travel through your mind. You may continue this experiment for as long a time as you desire, although a one hour maximum is recommended for safety reasons. Should you suddenly experience a compelling sense of fear, depression or anxiety, do not panic but immediately terminate the exercise.

STEP NO. 7

To conclude this amazing experiment, carefully follow each of the following guidelines without skipping over any of them:

1) Imagine yourself drifting in a blackened void.
2) Perform Step No. 5 in exact reverse.
3) Perform Step No. 3 in reverse.
4) Relax for about five minutes before resuming your normal activities.
5) Record the date and time of the experiment; also write down every possible detail you perceived in Step No. 6 for your own reference.

Believe it or not, the strange sounds and images you probably experienced in the course of the above experiment comprise actual memories of your past lives. With practice, you should be able to receive incredible impressions of this type with absolute clarity. And, if you persevere, it is possible to actually relive an entire past lifetime. You will be able to clearly know who you were, where and when you existed and the circumstances surrounding your life. To verify the overall validity of your impressions and thereby eliminate coincidence as well as imagination, all you need to do is review your history books. Check dates, places and conditions.

You may be amazed by what you find.

Chapter Nine

How To Find and Keep A Lover With ESP

Love is perhaps the most compelling force in the universe. It is man's redemption, yet his greatest pitfall. It may launch a person to the pinnacle of success or cause him to plummet the depths. We all crave companionship and affection, but few of us ever realize true happiness. Many of us have encountered numerous disappointments in romance.

If your love life in the past has been unfulfilling and you are in search of a more promising approach to the problem, continue reading and you may find an answer.

There is an easy way to avoid emotional crises. Arguments, broken love affairs and loneliness need not govern your existence. In fact, if you are willing to invest an inconsequential amount of time and energy, you can improve your prospects in romance beginning right now!

What's the secret?

ESP is your passport to happiness and success. This powerful agent is the key to a gratifying love life, the secret of enduring marriage. It has been locked away in your mind since the moment you were born. Unfortunately, you have failed to recognize the fact.

By applying the sensible easy-to-follow guidelines appearing in this chapter, you may take advantage of your hidden psychic power. You will learn how to attract people of the opposite sex, identify compatible lovers, find that one special "SOUL MATE" meant just for you, and establish a permanently rewarding relationship.

If you are currently married or involved in a floundering love affair, you may use ESP to alleviate tension, counteract deterioration, improve communication and drastically enrich your relationship in countless subtle ways that will contribute to mutual happiness.

Granted, these claims may seem fantastic, almost unbelievable. But you can confirm them to your own satisfaction. You have nothing to lose, and a new and more successful approach to romance may await you.

Once you discover the amazing effect ESP can have on your love life, you will probably want to kick yourself for not cultivating your hidden psychic power sooner.

THE SECRET OF PSYCHIC MAGNETISM

It is almost impossible to avoid contact with other men and women. In the course of day-to-day existence, we encounter scores of people, walking down the street, strolling through a park, or going to and from work and school.

Most are strangers that we may never see again. Yet, any one of them could be your "soul mate," and you would never suspect it. In fact, you may know such a person right now: a friend, neighbor, fellow employee, schoolmate or passing acquaintance.

The principal challenge confronting most of us then is that we must learn to recognize a compatible lover from amidst the multitude of nameless people we see each day. If we could only distinguish the right person, there would no longer be any reason for foolish errors in judgment that so often lead to disappointment and emotional breakdown.

How can one actually make such a distinction? Certainly, you cannot fall in love with everybody you meet until the ideal partner finally happens along. Neither can you dash up to a stranger on the street and administer a Rorschach Test. It is possible, though, to use extrasensory perception to judge potential lovers. To do this, you must familiarize yourself with a unique concept known as psychic magnetism.

This amazing concept eliminates the guesswork from your romantic affairs and permits you to obtain clear insights into a man or woman's true character. You can use the power to evaluate your relationships with present friends, coworkers, acquaintances, even strangers you meet in passing. Best of all, you do not need to exchange a single word to accomplish this enviable goal.

Psychic magnetism is based on the scientific maxim that like attracts like and opposites repel. Applied to your love life, this means that you are compatible with some people but in complete opposition with others. Let's face it:

No matter how hard you try, there are certain partners you could never get along with. Such individuals are not attuned to your mental wave length. Their emotional constitutions, needs and desires may conflict with your own and the essence of their personalities opposes yours. Living together in close quarters with such a mate would be a constant struggle, and in the final analysis the situation could become unbearable.

This explains why the divorce rate is so high today. People do not know how to tell whether they are in fact compatible. Once the glitter of romance has worn off, they come to realize the true magnitude of their differences and cannot make the necessary adjustments.

Fortunately, you may avoid making this fatal mistake by applying the secret of psychic magnetism. Using an easy technique you can evaluate a potential mate in minutes, any time and any place, without the person so much as suspecting. You will be able to determine who is really attuned to your wave length and distinguish those individuals from others who might prove to be disappointing. Then, when you have located a compatible lover, you may use psychic magnetism to kindle love at first sight and establish an enduring relationship that could prove to be the most gratifying experience of your lifetime.

How? Just observe the following step-by-step guidelines for utilizing this amazing natural phenomenon and you will be well on your way to ultimate happiness.

STEP NO. 1

Always keep your eyes open for likely prospects. Remain on the lookout whenever you are in public; during work or school, at informal social gatherings, while sitting on a park bench or dining at a restaurant. Carefully observe each and every person of the opposite sex you may encounter in the course of your day.

Note the individual's physical appearance: hair and eye color, facial features, complexion, clothing, height and weight. Then study his or her gestures and surface attitudes. Take notice of even the smallest details.

If you are even vaguely attracted by the person, proceed immediately to Step No. 2.

STEP NO. 2

Close your eyes and quickly blank all thought from your mind by using perfect relaxation. When the desired state has been achieved, perform standard visualization, constructing a clear and precise image of the person's face in your mind's eye. Maintain the image for approximately twenty to thirty seconds. This will enable you to establish a psychic link between the two of you and to reach out and momentarily touch minds.

Now, erase the picture from your mind and open your eyes again. Evaluate your emotional response toward the psychic contact which you established just seconds ago. Ask yourself—does this particular man (or woman) convey warmth and friendliness? Is there something cold or alien that you do not like about the person? Is the idea of intimately associating with him (or her) appealing? Or is there something ominous about the prospect of becoming involved in a deep relationship?

In carrying out this step, it is extremely important that you supply honest answers to each of the questions. You cannot expect to benefit from psychic magnetism if you attempt to deceive yourself. Therefore, be thorough and objective in the analysis of your feelings.

If you are not completely satisfied with your answers, you may rest assured that the person in question is on a different mental wave length than you. In other words, the two of you would most likely find a close relationship to be strained and, eventually, disappointing. Intimacy with such a person should therefore be avoided.

But if you still find that you are strongly attracted to this particular man or woman, go on to the next step without delay.

STEP NO. 3

If you have succeeded in reaching this step, it should be safe for you to assume that the person presently under scrutiny may be an ideal love mate and that a serious relationship could prove ultimately worthwhile. But before you dash up and introduce yourself, it would be advisable to determine whether the man or woman will respond favorably to your interest. It may be that you have singled out someone who is already married or involved in a love affair and has no further desire for romantic engagement. If that is so, it is best to utilize the following technique and find out beforehand.

Using the guidelines presented in Chapter Six, create an intense emotional thought form in your mind to suit the occasion; ideally, one of genuine warmth and affection. If you have not memorized the correct procedure, refer to the passage, "How To Create and Project Emotional Thought Forms," for complete instructions.

Once you have accomplished this step, inconspicuously lock gazes with the man or woman being evaluated. Hold the person's eyes for a few seconds and promptly transmit the prescribed thought form.

Carefully observe the individual's reaction: He or she should respond to this telepathic query almost instantly in one of several ways. Of course, to realize maximum benefit you must evaluate the response with complete objectivity. Don't permit wishful thinking to interfere with your better judgment.

STEP NO. 4

Having performed each of the preceding steps correctly, you should now be able to determine the prospective lover's availability; as well as clearly see whether or not the individual finds you personally appealing. His or her reaction to your emotional thought form provides the necessary clue.

To interpret the results of Step No. 3, just observe these guidelines:

If the man or woman refuses to meet eyes with you, it is an infallible indication that he or she is already preoccupied with an existing love relationship and has no desire to meet new people of the opposite sex. In order to prevent needless embarrassment on your own part, simply accept the fact and turn your attention to a more promising candidate.

If your emotional thought form is met by a frown or a look of disdain, it shows that the person in question *is* in the market for new social contacts but for one reason or another does *not* consider you to be appealing. This drawback could stem from any number of underlying causes, such as a recent bitter experience with romance or a past disappointment with a lover whose physical appearance strongly resembles your own. A subtle rejection of this sort does not necessarily imply a personal affront, but by the same token it is a clear indication that an intimate relationship between the two of you probably would not endure.

If, however, the man or woman meets your gaze and reacts interestedly, perhaps with a vague smile or a curious glance, it is a very promising sign. You already know that the individual is attuned to your mental wave length and therefore a compatible love mate; hence, this is one point in your favor. And this new evidence almost certainly suggests that he or she is unattached and looking for romantic involvement. Further, a favorable response such as this reveals that the person in question has carried out a hasty evaluation and decided that *you* are a promising prospect!

From this point on, it's up to you. Psychic magnetism can assist you in identifying prospective love mates ideally suited to you, but it cannot actually bring two people together. You must now rely upon your personality and your wits to make the first move and introduce yourself. But once you muster up the courage to follow 'through, you may be pleasantly surprised by the outcome. Many people no different from yourself have used psychic magnetism and realized astonishing results. You, too, may apply this secret to become united with your own "soul mate" and enter into a gratifying lifelong relationship.

Of course, there is more to a successful romance than using ESP to select a suitable partner. You must naturally be willing to give and take and exercise a measure of compassion in the course of daily living.

Always remember: Psychic magnetism is by no means the final answer to your every problem. But it may well be your passport to a fabulous love life.

HOW TO PRESERVE YOUR RELATIONSHIP—PSYCHICALLY

Beyond the subtle conflicts and tensions which may be anticipated in a love affair or married life, certain corrosive forces may demand your attention from time to time. A cantankerous relative opposed to your relationship, jealous friends and vengeful rivals often seek to interfere with your romantic harmony. Most of the time you will be able to contend with problems as they arise and quickly resolve them before the situation becomes a full-fledged crisis.

Yet, what can you do if a disgruntled friend or enemy tries using ESP to disrupt your love life? What if an envious rival attempts to psychically spy on you or implants offending telepathic suggestions in your mind?

Before you dismiss these possibilities as ridiculous, you must remember that thousands of people throughout the world are presently learning how to unlock their hidden psychic power. Unfortunately, not all may be altruistically inclined. As is true in most departments of life, there are bound to be a handful of unconscionable misfits who would not think twice about employing ESP to destroy a love relationship (or any other relationship).

Tragic but true, the threat of psychic attack is becoming more imminent with each passing day. And those motivated by revenge and jealousy are the most likely people to abuse ESP.

Fortunately, there is a way of identifying psychic attack at the onset and to prevent it from impending romantic harmony.

HOW TO IDENTIFY PSYCHIC ATTACK

Generally speaking, psychic aggression may take one of three distinct forms, each characterized by certain easy-to-identify symptoms.

The most common abuse, telepathic invasion, is usually more annoying than detrimental. It occurs when a jealous friend or rival employs mind reading to ascertain your innermost thoughts and feelings wholly against your will. This particular phenomenon is symptomized by constant ringing in the ears, dizziness, chronic headache originating in the region of the forehead and a general sense of mental discomfort.

Clairvoyant spying, which is the second most common infraction, entails your being observed by someone who is acquainted with the miracle of psychic television. The greatest inherent danger, especially in matters of love, is that a rival may utilize this extrasensory power to expose your private activities. This phenomenon is characterized by a sensation of constant weight on the chest and forehead, the feeling that someone is looking over your shoulder, and a sense of being watched wherever you may go.

The third variation entails outright mental assault by a rival or jilted lover. Photopic thought forms and the power of psychokinesis usually have an important role in this type of psychic attack. The principal danger is that an enemy could drain your vitality or implant subtle photopic suggestions in your mind, thereby causing you to think and behave in a potentially detrimental way, especially in romance. The symptoms of the phenomenon are varied: Sudden unexplained lack of energy, prolonged nausea, loss of appetite, unreasonable depression, diminished judgment and inability to exercise your free will are commonly reported characteristics. Also, ask yourself—Do I suddenly feel that life is not worth living without any justification? Am I prone to frequent fits of temper and erratic behavior? Does a foreign influence seem to be in control of my thoughts and actions?

Of course, it is practically impossible to know beyond a doubt that a psychic attack has been launched against you. Many of the symptoms described above could be caused by any number of unrelated circumstances. Unfortunately, by the time sufficient evidence has been amassed, it might be too late to initiate preventive measures. Therefore, in keeping with the worn but apt cliché that it is better to be safe than sorry, should the slightest indication of psychic assault become manifest, take the necessary steps to protect yourself. If you observe any of the symptoms in your lover or marriage partner, do the same. You may never be able to justify your suspicion, but you will be spared the trouble of finding out the hard way.

HOW TO COMBAT PSYCHIC ATTACK

There are several popular techniques which may be effectively implemented to combat the negative influence of a psychic attack. The ones presented here are the easiest and most efficacious means of preventing telepathic invasion, clairvoyant spying, and outright assault.

The first method requires retiring to a quiet room and attaining a state of complete tranquility by using perfect relaxation. Expel every thought and sensation from your mind. Envision nothing but a blackened void within and surrounding yourself. Maintain this condition for thirty minutes without interruption. If performed correctly, this simple exercise will frustrate unconscionable rivals and also cleanse your mind of any photopic suggestions which might have been implanted.

There is another simple technique. Surprising as it may seem, pain is a decided deterrent against all types of psychic assault. Therefore, all you must do is bite down hard on your lower lip or dig your fingernails into an arm until pain is evinced (but don't puncture the skin). Maintain the condition of physical discomfort for approximately thirty seconds to one minute, then resume your normal activities. This exercise is especially useful in obstructing telepathic invasion: The person who attempts to read your mind will perceive nothing but your pain and experience it himself. Hence, this is a sure way to discourage further intrusion!

Now that you know how to prevent psychic attack, use what you have learned whenever necessary. Both of the above techniques may be employed with minimal time and effort, so be certain to heed the first sign of danger and act promptly. You may never need to apply this newly-acquired knowledge. But if such a time ever comes, you will be able to preserve your love relationship as well as your peace of mind.

HOW TO ENRICH YOUR LOVE AFFAIR (OR MARRIAGE)

Two lovers in close association are bound to experience petty conflicts and misunderstandings. This is an inescapable fact. Yet, we can use ESP to reduce subtle tensions and fortify our relationships. Properly applied, your hidden psychic power may prevent minor difficulties from developing into major proportions and thereby insure lifelong happiness free from the dilemma of broken love affairs and divorce.

Here are some practical guidelines for taking advantage of your extrasensory gifts to build a mutually gratifying relationship:

1) Cultivate mind-to-mind communication with your mate. Practice, and this ability will unfold naturally. You will then be able to exchange ideas, thoughts and deep emotion with great ease. Telepathy is really quite superior to normal speech, for it enables you to always express yourself simply, clearly and effectively.

2) Never use ESP to spy on your partner's thoughts and activities. If you suspect that he or she is unfaithful, get your information some other way. Psychic spying invariably leads to resentment and could easily compound the original problem.

3) However, if your mate seems unusually troubled by something or succumbs to deep depression, *do* use ESP to determine the root of the problem. But do *not* be forceful or overbearing. If you are gentle and discreet, the situation should surely become resolved to your best interests.

4) Whenever you or your lover are apart, you

should occasionally project an emotional thought form of deep affection. This will dispel loneliness and confirm your true feelings toward one another. It is also an ideal way to remain psychically in contact and keep your love intact, no matter how much distance may come between you.

The guidelines presented in this chapter may assist you in realizing many tremendous advantages in your love life. But you must apply this knowledge, follow all directions exactly and seriously believe in the value of ESP if you want it to work for you.

With practice and the right mental attitude, you will surely come to find that your hidden psychic power is indeed your passport to happiness in love.

Chapter Ten

How To Test Your ESP

Having read the preceding chapters, you should now be thoroughly acquainted with the unique psychic powers at your disposal. Hopefully, the tremendous value of extrasensory perception has been impressed firmly upon your mind.

If you have taken the time to practice the growth exercises related earlier and followed the step-by-step guidelines for personal development, you will be well on your way to mastering ESP and using your sixth sense in all daily affairs. The powers of telepathy, clairvoyance, psychokinesis and precognition, if properly applied, may enable you to realize your innermost desires and insure your ultimate happiness and fulfillment as you progress through the weeks and months ahead. Thousands of people are now cultivating their hidden psychic powers, and if you have decided to take advantage of your own inborn abilities, you should never have cause for regret. Indeed, ESP, used constructively, is one of the most positive, gratifying powers in the universe.

Through a series of simple tests designed to reveal your current level of psychic development, you may discover how well you have learned some of the techniques presented in this book. These tests will point out possible deficiencies in your development and suggest areas, if any, that require further refinement.

There are various ways of testing extrasensory power, some more revealing and accurate than others. The tests presented here are the standard ones used by the majority of parapsychologists and ESP researchers throughout the country. To administer them, just follow directions and avoid feeling pressured. Remember, you are not competing with anyone.

To maintain a meaningful record of your progress in the months and years ahead, you should undergo complete re-testing every sixty days. This will enable you to not only chart your psychic growth, but to determine whether you have permitted any of your extrasensory powers to deteriorate through lack of use. Hence, through occasional re-evaluation, you will insure that you remain in peak psychic condition at all times.

HOW TO TEST YOUR ESP

The GESP (General Extrasensory Perception) test battery which follows is a complete set of standard tests for telepathy, clairvoyance, psychokinesis, precognition and retrocognition.

To perform this series, you will need a pen or

pencil, paper, a set of dice, a deck of regular playing cards, and a deck of standard Rhine Cards. The latter, devised by Dr. J. B. Rhine, may be purchased for a nominal price at most larger bookstores, and at certain novelty shops or pharmacies. If you cannot obtain a deck in your hometown, you can make a homemade version.

To do this, you must have a package of opaque index cards or some other type of thick cardboard which can be cut into squares. The Rhine card deck consists of twenty-five cards, divided into five suits. Therefore, draw each of these designs on five cards, using black ink: star, square, circle, cross (+), and wavy lines. Make each symbol dark and be sure all the markings are precise and legible. Also, it is important that the cardboard be thick enough so you cannot see through to the image; otherwise, the validity of the tests will automatically be nullified. Shuffle the deck well, and it is ready for use.

In conducting the GESP test battery, you will need the cooperation of a friend, since it is impossible to administer some parts of the series to yourself. Your assistant does not need to be psychically developed, and since the complete battery should consume no more than an hour, you will probably not encounter difficulty in enlisting the aid of a likely candidate.

When you are ready to begin, seat yourself at a table facing your partner. Use perfect relaxation to subdue your body, but at this point it is not necessary to blank your mind of thoughts. Your partner should be in possession of the cards, dice and other equipment. He or she should also be given pen and paper to keep track of your score.

TESTING FOR TELEPATHY

Instruct your partner to number a sheet of paper from one to twenty-five in a vertical column. Then, tell him to pick up the top Rhine card on the deck and gaze at the symbol on its face, forming and maintaining a vivid image of the design in his mind's eye. Your objective is to determine the correct symbol.

Blank your mind and try to receive the thought being sent to you. When you are certain of the answer, call it aloud. Your partner should then record your statement on paper, placing beside it the correct symbol. Do not concern yourself with whether your guess was correct, and don't glance at your partner's notation. Simply continue with the test.

Repeat the same procedure until you have called all twenty-five Rhine cards. At the end of the run, have your partner count the number of correct answers, placing the score at the bottom of the column.

Perform this entire step again until you have made three runs through the deck. Then, determine your average score by adding all the scores together and dividing by three. For example:

$$\begin{aligned}
&\text{Run 1 Score— 8 correct}\\
&\text{Run 2 Score—10 correct}\\
&\text{Run 3 Score— 9 correct}
\end{aligned}$$

TOTAL SCORE—27 correct
AVERAGE   — 9 (27 divided by 3)

Next, evaluate your average:

16-25 — Superior
12-15 — Very good
10-11 — Good
6- 9 — Fair
0- 5 — Poor

TEST FOR CONTACT TELEPATHY

To perform this test, instruct your assistant to take one of the dice and hide it in another room of your house. You should be given no clues as to the correct location. When your friend returns, take his hand into your own and employ the power of contact telepathy (as taught in Chapter One) to locate the concealed die. If you succeed in determining the hiding place in two minutes or less, rate your ability as "excellent." If it requires up to four minutes, your rating is "good." However, if more than four minutes is required, or if you fail to locate the concealed object, your rating is "poor," and it would be advisable for you to re-develop this power or it may altogether deteriorate.

TESTING FOR CLAIRVOYANCE (STANDARD PSYCHIC VISION)

For this section of the GESP test battery, you will need a pen, paper and Rhine cards.

Instruct your partner to shuffle the deck thoroughly, then number a sheet of paper from one to twenty-five as was done in the test for telepathy. Have him place the Rhine cards face down in the middle of the table.

Your objective is to use the miracle of psychic television to determine which symbol is on the face of the first card, without either you or your partner knowing the correct answer in advance. Use standard psychic vision to actually see the face of the first card in your mind's eye. When you are sure of the answer, verbally state it. Your friend should record your call, then pick up the first card and mark down the correct answer without letting you see it, just as was done in the telepathy test.

Use the same technique to call the remaining cards. At the conclusion of the run, instruct your assistant to count the number of correct answers and insert your score at the bottom of the column.

Repeat this procedure until you have performed a total of three runs through the deck. Determine your average score by combining the number of points from all the runs and dividing by three, as you did in the test for telepathy.

Now evaluate your average score:

17-25 — Superior
14-16 — Very good
10-13 — Good
6- 9 — Fair
0- 5 — Poor

TESTING FOR PRECOGNITION

This section of the GESP battery is designed to measure your latent precognitive ability. It is not a test of how vividly future impressions register, but rather of your accuracy in interpreting insights obtained through this faculty.

Instruct your partner to administer this test by following the same procedure used to evaluate telepathic ability. As he or she concentrates on the first card in the deck you must close your eyes. Several symbols will enter your mind: a vague one first, then a clear one followed by another weak design. Ignore all but the first and call it aloud. Using this procedure, complete the full run through the deck.

At the conclusion of three runs, tell your friend to determine your rating by crediting one point for each symbol called correctly *one card in advance*. For example, the following diagram indicates four correct calls:

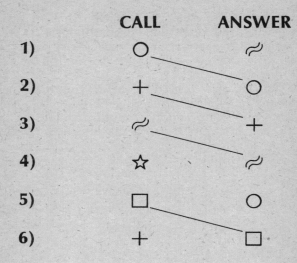

	CALL	ANSWER

Now, combine the total points in each run and divide that number by three to arrive at your overall average. Determine your personal evaluation by consulting the scoring table in the section, "Testing For Clairvoyance (Standard Psychic Vision)."

TESTING FOR LATENT RETROCOGNITION

This, the fifth section of the GESP series, is concerned primarily with rating your latent retrocognitive ability.

In administering this particular test, observe the same basic guidelines given in the preceding section on precognition. Have your partner concentrate intently on the first card. At the same time close your eyes. Once again, you should be able to perceive a weak symbol, then a clear one and another weaker design. *Ignore the first two symbols*, and call the third one aloud. When your friend has recorded your score, follow the same procedure to complete the run.

Once you have completed a total of three full runs through the deck, tell your assistant to compute your score by crediting one point for each symbol called correctly *one card later*. The standard procedure is just the reverse of the one used for precognition.

Now, combine the total points for each run and divide the resulting figure by three to ascertain your overall average. Consult the scoring table in the section, "Testing for Clairvoyance (Standard Psychic Vision)."

TESTING FOR PSYCHOKINESIS

Section Six of the GESP Battery permits you to accurately measure the extent of your psychokinetic power; that is to say, your ability to exercise mind over matter. The test requires a set of dice, so put the Rhine cards aside.

Have your partner number a sheet of paper from one to twenty-five. Then, you must call out any two numbers between one and six. Your partner should record these digits, then take both dice into his hand.

Using the method cited in Chapter Five your task is to cause both the die to fall on those numbers you selected. Concentrate on this goal. When ready, tell your partner to toss the dice. Your score should be recorded alongside the two numbers that you called.

Repeat this exact procedure for a total of

twenty-five throws, the equivalent of one run. Then, perform two further runs to complete the test.

To score this section, instruct your partner to credit you with 1 point if you correctly called one dice in a single throw, and 2½ points if both the dice fell as desired. For example:

	Your Call	Your Answer	Point Total
1)	6 - 2	2 - 5	1
2)	5 - 5	5 - 4	1
3)	4 - 2	1 - 1	0
4)	3 - 4	3 - 4	2½
5)	1 - 5	5 - 1	2½
6)	6 - 4	4 - 1	1

Now, compute the total for each of the three runs and place your score at the bottom of the column. To find your overall average, combine the scores of each of the runs and divide this number by three. Based on the resulting total, evaluate yourself:

53 - 62½	—	Superior
44 - 52	—	Very Good
28 - 43	—	Good
18 - 27	—	Fair
0 - 17	—	Poor

TESTING FOR PENETRATIVE CLAIRVOYANCE

In this test, your power of penetrative clairvoyance, (x-ray vision) will be rated. To perform it, you must have a deck of regular playing cards. Have your assistant remove the tens, jacks, queens, kings and aces from the deck. (The remaining cards should be placed aside.) Have him shuffle these cards well and then place them face down on the table.

Instruct your partner to pick up the top card and, without looking, drop it into a small metal or wooden box with a lid. Once this is done, the top of the container should be shut tightly.

Your objective now is to use the power of penetrative clairvoyance to determine the color of the card, as well as the suit and denomination (for example: red, queen, diamond). To best accomplish this, use the technique revealed to you in Chapter Three.

When you are sure of the answer, call it aloud. Your friend should then record your response, open the container and determine the correct answer. This, too, should be written down.

Perform this exact procedure a total of ten times, then instruct your partner to credit points for correct answers in the following way: 1 point per accurate color response (red or black), 2½ points per accurate suit response (heart, spade, diamond, club), and 2½ points per correct denomination of each card (ten, jack, queen, king, ace).

For example:

Your Call	Answer	Point Value
1) Red, Jack, Diamond	Red, Jack, Heart	3½
2) Black, Ace, Spade	Black, Ace, Spade	6
3) Black, Queen, Club	Black, King, Spade	1
4) Red, Ten, Diamond	Black, Jack, Club	0
5) Black, King, Club	Red, King, Diamond	2½

Now, compute your total score by combining all the points received on each of the ten calls. The resulting digit represents your present psychokinetic ability. To evaluate your score, use the preceding table you used for the psychokinesis test.

CONCENTRATION TEST

The importance of ultra-concentration must never be underrated. Virtually every ESP talent relies heavily on your ability to focus your mind on a single thought or object without interference. Hence, if you lack concentration, your psychic potential will necessarily be diminished.

The following written test has been reproduced from Chapter Two so that it will be possible for you to maintain an accurate check on your power of concentration. The scoring method, however, is slightly different from the one appearing earlier in that it is more stringent.

Before answering the questions, perform this simple exercise. Place a regular playing card before you and focus your complete attention on the number in the right-hand corner. Instruct your partner to time you, and let him know when you begin to concentrate.

At the end of a full three minutes, conclude the exercise, and answer the following questions. Remember, it is extremely important that you respond honestly at all times. Review each question carefully in your mind, then mark "yes" or "no."

1) While performing the above exercise, did you experience restlessness to a substantial degree?

2) Did your mind have a tendency to wander?

3) Was it difficult for you to concentrate in the prescribed manner for the entire three minutes?

4) Did you experience:
   a) Cramped Muscles?
   b) Nausea?
   c) Headache?
   d) Other discomfort?
5) Did noise, movement or other nearby commotion interrupt your concentration?
6) Do you believe you are out of shape?

Give yourself one point for each "yes" answer and then evaluate your total:

0	— Superior
1	— Good
2	— Fair
3 or higher	— Poor

How well did you do? If you failed to pass this test, you are probably scoring below average on the remainder of the GESP test battery. This is not because you lack psychic potential, but rather due to your inability to concentrate properly. If this happens to be the case, review the appropriate passages in Chapter Two, then undergo re-testing and you will notice a drastic improvement in your scores.

STANDARD VISUALIZATION TEST

In this, the final section of the GESP battery, you will be able to accurately determine your capacity for using the technique of standard visualization.

To administer this test, simply place a regular playing card, ideally the king of clubs, before you. Using the standard visualization technique, your goal is to maintain a clear and exact image of the card in your mind's eye for a full five minutes.

When you are ready to begin, instruct your partner to time you. Then, employ visualization. If, in the process of this test, the mental image becomes blurred, discolored or otherwise distorted, or begins to fade away before the specified time has passed, terminate the exercise immediately and have your assistant record the exact number of minutes and seconds consumed from the start. Again, it is extremely important that you be honest with yourself; if your visualizing is not up to par, this fact should be noted and your technique refined for maximum success in future endeavors.

If you are able to maintain the image for the entire five minute time span, there is no need to repeat this section of the GESP series; however, if you encounter difficulty at first, you may make up to three tries and base your rating on the best. Evaluate yourself:

> 5 minutes — Superior
> 4 - 5 minutes — Good
> 3 - 4 minutes — Fair

HOW TO RECORD
YOUR GESP TEST RESULTS

Having concluded the entire GESP test battery, you should now make a permanent record of your scores. In this way, you will be able to accurately chart your progress in the months and years ahead. Naturally, it is not necessary to retain all the score sheets and notations compiled by your partner, but the overall results should be recorded and filed for future reference. The "GESP Profile Sheet" at the end of this chapter is ideally suited to this purpose. It is a convenient reference form that enables you to compare current test scores with previous ones at a glance.

A SPECIAL WORD ABOUT THIS TEST

The principal intent of the GESP test battery, and any other developmental quiz, is to measure your current psychic potential. Yet, no matter how many precautions are observed, it is impossible to guarantee the accuracy of the results. Many subtle factors must be taken into consideration, but none other is quite so influential as the element of human psychology.

This is the most serious drawback encountered not only in laboratory experiments of a parapsychological nature but also in applying such tests as the GESP battery: ESP is not always a tangible thing that can be studied under a microscope. If a person is not in a susceptible frame of mind, or if emotional crises are foremost in the mind, psychic sensitivity may be impeded and a low score is then almost inevitable.

Another factor which frequently negates the validity of scientific evaluation is the average individual's overwhelming and intrinsic fear of failure. Practically every man, woman and child alive is driven by a compulsion to demonstrate competence in all undertakings. Far too often, the desire for success leads to psychological tension and stress which work together to invariably defeat the very objective being sought.

The truth of this statement is clearly illustrated by some students and prospective employees who may be quite gifted. Yet, given a test form and a pencil, they seem altogether unable to exercise simple logic or to correctly respond to the most obvious questions.

If you happen to be one of those people who

simply cannot function in a test situation, it is quite likely that your score in the GESP battery will fall short of your true psychic power. Extrasensory perception works best under tranquil conditions; you can't force yourself and hope to achieve meaningful results. Nevertheless, don't be discouraged. As time passes, you will become more accustomed to these ESP quizzes and your true abilities will begin to show through.

Always remember: The important thing is not how well you score on a telepathy test, but how successfully you employ your sixth sense in day-to-day existence. A high score is totally meaningless unless you put your talents to work along constructive, practical lines.

Make use of your powers and remain confident of your success. Be enthusiastic but not overanxious.

Therein lies the secret of psychic mastery.

GESP PROFILE SHEET

Subject's Name: Alice P. Doe Date: 4/1/73
Assistant: Margaret Smith Time: 12:30 PM

Test Classification	Average Score	Rating
Telepathy	15	Very good
Contact telepathy	3 minutes	Good
Psychic vision	9	Fair
Precognition	13	Good
Retrocognition	15	Superior
Psychokinesis	15	Poor
Penetrative clairvoyance	53	Superior
Concentration power	1	Good
Standard visualization	4.5 minutes	Good

Comments:

Assistant's Verification   Signature

Chapter Eleven

Psychic Power:
Your Key To Happiness and Success

With the information contained in these chapters, you should be able to cultivate your sixth sense and use it to the fullest extent. But you must practice to develop your hidden psychic power, then practice to maintain your abilities.

ESP, if properly applied, may prove to be your passport to happiness and success. It can be used to enrich your love life, benefit your career pursuits and provide you with tremendous insights into yourself, your friends and loved ones, and the surrounding universe.

Having studied this text and mastered the easy techniques presented within, you are now ready to embark on a new, more rewarding path through life and achieve your innermost dreams.

Good luck, and may you be ESPecially successful!